Roots of Violence
in the U.S. Culture

Roots of Violence
in the
U.S. Culture

A Diagnosis Towards Healing

ALAIN J. RICHARD

Foreword by Richard Rohr

Blue Dolphin Publishing

Published by Blue Dolphin Publishing, Inc.
P.O. Box 8, Nevada City, CA 95959
Orders: 1-800-643-0765
Web: www.bluedolphinpublishing.com

ISBN: 1-57733-043-9

Library of Congress Cataloging-in-Publication Data

Richard, Alain, J., 1925–
    Roots of violence in the U.S. culture : a diagnosis towards healing /
Alain J. Richard.
        p.   cm.
    Includes bibliographical references.
    ISBN: 1-57733-043-9 (alk. paper)
    1. Violence—United States.   2. Capitalism—Moral and ethical
aspects—United States.   3. United States—Social conditions—
1980–   I. Title.
HN90.V5R53   1999
303.6'0973—dc21   99-44850
                                                              CIP

Cover design: Lito Castro

Printed in the United States of America

10   9   8   7   6   5   4   3   2   1

To all my American friends,
with gratitude for
twenty-five years spent in their midst.

"*Nothing is more embarrassing in the ordinary intercourse of life*
than this irritable patriotism of the Americans.
A stranger may be well inclined to praise
many of the institutions of their country,
but he begs permission to blame some things in it,
a permission that is inexorably refused.
America is therefore a free country in which,
lest anybody should be hurt by your remarks,
you are not allowed to speak freely of private individuals or
of the state, of the citizens, or of the authorities,
of public or of private undertakings, or in short, of anything at all
except, perhaps, the climate and the soil; and even then
Americans will be found ready to defend both
as if they had co-operated in producing them"

Alexis de Tocqueville, *The Democracy in America*, 1831, p. 244

Contents

Foreword

I ONCE HEARD IMAGINATION, especially religious imagination, described as "intellect plus will—squared"! This is probably why most great religious teachers did not just give you facts, information, and pep-talks, but instead tried to subvert and transform your essential imaginal world. Until that happens, religion remains all in the head—where it can easily be forgotten, changed by new information, or used to bludgeon other people. But it does not transform.

No wonder that many people see the history of religion as a history of guiltless violence and a clever guise for remaining inside one's own tiny comfort zone. So different than the *good* and truly *new* places that God led people like Moses, Jesus, Gandhi, Dorothy Day, and the many other women who had no other way to "withdraw and lead" except through the mystical journey. But these good new places were also dangerous and uncharted territory for most of human history. Without God, no one would go there.

In this brilliant "diagnosis," my brother Alain Richard gives us the needed "facts and information" so we can both *allow and ask for* the utterly new imagination that is needed today. Unless and until we "get out of the way" with our illusions, there is no way that God's new agenda has a chance of being heard. The roots of violence that are described in this book will help both the reader and the dominant culture to get out of the way.

The role of the prophet usually has to precede the role of the priest. The prophet must deconstruct the false images before the priest can fittingly present the true images and expect them to be received. The prophet guides us on the necessary but always avoided "path of the fall," while the priest guides us toward *the encounter itself.* What we have today in most Christian churches is a lot of "priesthood" but very little prophecy. We have no radically new place or Person to encounter because we have never left the false comforts of home base. Priesthood without prophecy is almost always self-serving and very often in service of imperial religion and violent culture. Alain is honest enough in this book to present us with a modest but necessary goal. He does not venture into the "remedies to violence," but prophetically gives us a clear diagnosis in order to free us from our blind and addictive trance. Like John the Baptist, he levels the playing field so we can see how power, patriotism, and possessions are really in control.

Probably it takes someone from outside our North American culture (who yet loves what is good in this culture) to see what we cannot see and say what we cannot say. This "diagnosis toward healing" is a necessary first step out of our collective sleep walk, the kind of broad and contemplative seeing that a truly "catholic" church should be offering to our violent and contentious world. Too often the church only mirrors the power patterns of the system, instead of offering a true alternative.

It seems to me important, therefore, that this deconstruction comes from inside the religious community; and I am especially proud that it is coming from a Franciscan confrere. The Bible itself has been described as a slow and tedious "overcoming of the violence in God." It could be argued that religion itself has been the justification for much of the blindness and violence in human history. Instead of leading history to a *transformed seeing,* we in religion have used God to prop up our own cultural needs and power agendas. As Jesus put it, with extraordinary insight, "Because you say 'We see,' your guilt remains" (John 9:41). The world was once offered a God bigger than tribal religion, Yahweh the God of *all* the earth. Jesus honored this God, but much of Christian history has remained comfortable with tribalism and exclusion, which always leads to "sacralized" violence. By sacred violence we mean religion's common attempt to expel the contaminating element, instead of healing, forgiveness, and reconciliation with "the enemy," including and transforming the supposed contaminating element.

Religion is either the best thing in the world, when it leads to true union with God, creation, and ourselves—or it is often the very worst thing in the world, leading to expulsion and illusion. Our brother, Francis of Assisi, showed us "the Jesus way" of simplicity and non-violence, but we ourselves were often so trapped in our cultures that we were somehow able to debunk and avoid both Jesus and Francis, while still calling them our teachers and fathers. Really, quite amazing! It seems that the safest way to avoid the message is to "worship" the messenger. For some reason it frees us from the guilt of not really listening to them.

I live among the Franciscan missions of New Mexico, where we are still carrying the blame for imperialistic religion after 400 years, as is true in much of the Americas. Of course, the "blame game" is a dead end and usually a way to avoid our own transformation. We do not want to get trapped in victimization ourselves, or we will only continue the *quid pro quo,* tit for tat mentality that has controlled most of human history. Many activists, thinking they are enlightened, are still wasting most of their time looking for the "bad guys" to now victimize in reverse—because they are now deemed to be the *true* oppressors! Nothing has really changed, and this is not a new agenda, and yet it dangerously poses as one! All it does is change the characters and stage positions, but the plot line remains the same: *Who are we now allowed to hate and attack in return?* There has been no progress, and we have merely become mirror images of those we now deem to be inferior. It is the same old ego still jockeying for position. We are ready to move to a more mature spiritual consciousness, I think.

Einstein said, "No problem can be solved within the same consciousness that caused it." What healthy religion gives us is an authentically new consciousness, a creative "third something" beyond fight or flight, beyond liberal correctness and conservative righteousness, beyond again dividing the world into the good guys (which *we* always happen to be) and the bad guys (whom we are allowed to justifiably expel, imprison, torture, and kill). Mere liberal ideology has shown itself incapable of overcoming this scapegoating mechanism in this century. It only scapegoats, expels, and hates in a more hidden and sophisticated way than the traditional cultures did (witness the violent political correctness of leftist communism, market economics, and some radical feminism). It seems that human beings need, want, and desire to place the problem *elsewhere*. Anything, anything at all, to avoid my own transformation!

It seems that culture—every culture—is inherently self-protective of its own self-interest and its own power structures. Unless there is some Transcendent Reference Point that reveals the lie, most of us remain trapped within our own self-serving logic. Religion called this "conversion." I like to call it true transformation, or the movement from the calculating mind to the contemplative mind. Whatever we call it, it is a gift from God that leaves us both *free from* our cultural logic, and yet also *free to* enter back into our culture with compassion, mercy, and non-violence. It seems to be a participation in the very patience and mind of God.

Until our very minds and hearts are freed from violence, freed from the very need to scapegoat anybody or create victims anywhere, we will not be any kind of "new creation." Until we can seek win/win situations, we are not at all usable for God. Too often when Christians use "victory" language, they are still inside of win/lose scenarios. Religion is just a cosmic super bowl, and the important thing is to beat the enemy. No time for win/win situations; in fact, it does not even feel very attractive to most "combatants."

We wade through the Bible itself, seemingly two steps forward and three steps backward, until only at the end of the Gospels do we arrive at a non-violent image of God: The Risen Jesus. He blames nobody; he punishes no one. He doesn't even bring it all up: the betrayals, the abandonment, the torture, the unfaithfulness of almost everybody. Instead, he identifies forgiveness and peace with his very breath— constant, quiet, unearned—but always given (John 20:20-22). Perhaps the slow journey of the whole Bible parallels our own slow human transformation. It takes us a long time to get to non-violence, it seems. I am told that the very words did not exist in most languages until the 1960s, yet the practice is obvious in the truly great religious teachers. Our consciousness was not ready.

If the Risen Jesus is the true image of the nature of God, then finally, it has become a safe world. God is not violent, and religion is no longer a threat, nor can it achieve its purposes through threat, domination, punishment, or coercion. Grace and mercy don't work that way. But our consciousness was not ready yet.

Now we can no longer just give answers and explanations, we have to *become* the answer, and our own transformation is the only credible explanation. It seems we must tame and integrate the demon of violence within ourselves before we have anything to say to anybody else. Such work for justice will not merely rearrange the same old furniture, but will invite us to share with God in building a whole new house. It is all invitation. God only needs fitting images, it seems.

I think human consciousness has moved beyond its collective teenager stage: group think, win/lose scenarios, "redemptive" violence, religion as threat and punishment. We are finally ready to talk about free gifts and divine invitations.

Richard Rohr, OFM
Center for Action & Contemplation
Albuquerque, New Mexico

Preface

I AM AN ADMIRER OF THE PEOPLE of the United States. Nevertheless, after spending 25 years in the U.S., I have become concerned about some manifestations of the North American culture. This book is an attempt to search out the roots of violence specific to the North American culture. I recognize that this is a very ambitious project. Violence is everywhere and has diverse origins. Some roots of violence are the direct result of the mysterious contradictions within the human being. Violence comes from human nature itself, especially the propensity to imitate, as René Girard and Gil Bailie pointed out. Violence comes from religious patterns, from historical rivalries, from structures of thinking, and from social structures. Western culture provokes special violences; capitalism and communism each bring specific violences. **This analysis, however, is limited to the North American Way of Life.** Reflecting upon events in which I have personally been involved, in this text I examine the North American culture and explore its core for particular roots of violence. The matter is extremely complex as cultural principles are established not by an assembly or a decree, but little by little, and influenced by a multitude of events or forces.

After an introduction, definitions will be given in Chapter 1; then examples of unrealized promising possibilities within the U.S.A. in Chapter 2. In Chapter 3, the notion of market culture will be developed together with its emergence and how it eliminates the recognition of the sacredness dwelling inside each creature. This undisclosed violence is of incredible magnitude. The market culture grew out of a complex set of causes and principles. Some of its principles were created and developed by the colonial origin of the U.S. culture. For this reason the seeds of violence which can be traced to the country's colonial origin will be considered in Chapter 4, focusing on a) the depth of the racism grounded in the culture, b) the belief in a messianic role, c) the importance in the North American psyche of being "Number One," and d) the imperial policy of the country. Relationships will be drawn among these various seeds and the developing of the market culture.

Chapter 5 is a reflection on the frustrated dreams that originated in the culture. The market culture presents as a value the immediate satisfaction of a growing number of desires. When immediate satisfaction is impossible, frustration can lead to extreme violence. The myth of the American dream that did not materialize for a large minority creates for many a deep frustration. Similarly, the myth of a messianic mission given to the North American nation brings frustration and violence when it is perceived as unfulfilled.

Then my reflection will center on the special type of individualism represented by the *self-made man*, an important role model (Chapter 6). This model impedes man from reaching wholeness and brings to him a deep frustration. Moreover, the truncated anthropology that gave birth to the self-made man helped develop the market society as the communitarian barriers established by religions and humanisms broke apart.

In Chapter 7, I will attempt to gather the various interactions of the roots of violence, mainly market culture and wounded anthropology. My opinion is that their interaction, which happened in a colonial context, gave birth to the very special violence of the American culture.

All along the way I will give glimpses as to how a nonviolent spirit and technique could heal the ubiquitous violence that I describe. However, this book is not about the remedies to violence. People impatient to change the situation too often choose remedies before they have enough clarity on what needs to be healed. This book limits its exploration to the roots of violence specific to the U.S. Way of Life. Other writings by field activists or by scholars will need to give more details about the possibilities of nonviolence for changing the American Way of Life. We know that making a culture respectful of humanness and sacredness can be only done slowly. My confidence in the nonviolent process as the best way, for such a transformation is built on a multitude of facts of the past and indices for future use. In this book I will only briefly advance a few directions for reflection in an Afterword, so as not to distract from the main focus—the cultural roots of violence in the U.S. culture.

I warmly express my very special thanks to the PACE E BENE team which encouraged me to write this book and helped me with counsel along the way. The main thoughts of this book ripened during our nine years of work and reflection together.

For the choices concerning the content of this writing I owe very much to lengthy exchanges with Barry Stenger, Ph.D, Robert Lasalle, Ph.D, Louis Vitale, Ph.D, Peter Ediger, D.Min, and Sr.Rosemary Lynch, OSF. Peter Ediger patiently helped me all along the writing process to clarify my thoughts, challenging them sometimes, and graciously accepting to be challenged by my make-up and my way of looking at American realities.

Joan Brown, Mike Affleck, Stevi Carroll, Richard Lewnau, Brendan Mc Keague, and others agreed to read certain chapters and offered significant editorial improvements.

The tedious work of editing has been done patiently by Sr. Michele Ficher, Sr.Rosemary Lynch, and Peter Ediger, to whom I am grateful for their efforts in correcting my many French expressions. If some of them remained it is not their fault but my stubbornness in preferring unusual ways that I found more faithful to my thinking.

I also received competent and valuable remarks from Teofilo Argueta Ramirez, Licenciado en Filosofia, from the Kino Institute in Phoenix, John Kavanaugh, S.J. professor of Ethics at St. Louis University, Patricia M. Mische from Global Education Associates, Joe Nangle, OFM, Kenan Osborn, OFM, Professor of Theology and Franciscan Spirituality at the Franciscan School of Theology in Berkeley, and Barry Stenger from Santa Clara University. I am grateful for their friendship in giving me some of their precious time.

And may my gratefulness find wings to reach,
wherever they may be,
all those who taught me by words and example
that the dignity of the human being is not for sale.

Roots of Violence
in the U.S. Culture

Introduction

WHEN I SETTLED IN THE UNITED STATES with a green card in 1973, I had not been sent by the King of France, as Alexis de Tocqueville the French social observer had been in 1831, in order to write a report. I was almost twice his age when I arrived in an extremely poor area of Chicago. Some of my Franciscan brothers had asked me to join them in their community life and ministry in their rough neighborhood. Writing was not my purpose for coming to Chicago; I had come to follow more fully my inner call to live the Gospel in the midst of the poor. If I had anything in common with Tocqueville, other than my French origin, it was my admiration for the North American people,[1] which is still very high.

Tocqueville had been drawn to the United States of America out of an interest in equality.[2] My special attraction was the freedom of this country and its inhabitants. To me it seemed that people here were not enslaved by old patterns of thinking and doing. Was such liberty and creativity still alive and well? Was the United States of America still the land where everything was possible with no barrier of routine or incongruity? Was tolerance still practiced in all areas of life? These were some of the questions I was eager to explore through sharing life with searching brothers who settled in the midst of the poor.

Many images were very alive in my memory when I arrived: long years of friendship between American and French people, Lafayette, the Louisiana purchase—many enthusiastic remarks by Tocqueville based on his discoveries about America. The famous sentence "Lafayette, nous voilà" ("Lafayette, we are here!") of U.S. soldiers arriving during World War I was resounding in my ears. Very close to me were the gigantic efforts of this country preparing the Debarkment Day to free Europe from Nazism; the first American troops that I saw liberating the North of France; the embraces of American soldiers on the Champs Elysées in Paris, and many more images, some of which were true, while others proved to be clichés.

Today, twenty-five years after my arrival in the U.S.A., I am reflecting on my experiences in Chicago, Oakland, and for the last nine years Las Vegas. I continue to be amazed by the wide and varied possibilities of the North American context. My long stay in California was especially instructive to me in that respect .

Yet, during these twenty-five years I have seen so many possibilities, so many wonderful promises, so many hopes wither or vanish. Why? Why did so many blossoms of the past not open and bear fruit? Why do so many realities of the present lead young people to cynicism and violence? Why do so many dashed expectations leave a bitter taste of deception? Many incriminate the political or economic system or the politicians of the opposite party. Some place the responsibility on international events, others on economic conditions, or they credit other causes. To me it seems obvious that powerful realities of the culture strangled many of the promising new blossoms. Structures of the dominant culture did not leave any space for these new hopes; the blossoms of hope withered, and disappeared. My reflections on the North American culture are certainly shaped by my French heritage. For example, shortly after settling in the United States, a torrential rain severely damaged the Mississippi Basin and the flood destroyed an important bridge. The newspaper headline struck me "An X Million Dollar Bridge Destroyed." Only further down did the article mention that this sudden destruction inconvenienced some 200,000 people. In my country I would have read: "200,000 People Inconvenienced by the Destruction of a Bridge." Of course the amount of money requested for rebuilding would have been mentioned afterwards, possibly because such an amount of money would mean more delay for rebuilding, thus lengthening the inconvenience. On many other occasions in news reports, I have read or heard amounts of money noted, and only as an afternote, the repercussions upon human beings.

My perspective on North America is shaped not only by my life in France, but also by many cross-cultural experiences. Participation in various short term projects for nonviolent action and human rights in Central America and Sri Lanka has led me to fruitful comparisons between different cultures of Third World countries and the North American culture. These experiences have helped me see that within the U.S. culture there is the presence of specific sources of violence.

Nine years ago a few companions and I started the **Pace e Bene Center** in Las Vegas. As a Franciscan service in nonviolence, Pace e Bene, through its modest contribution, works toward the transformation of the U.S. culture. Our intuition was and still is that violence in the United States of America is not mainly the result of personal, economic, or political choices made at a specific time of history, but that it has deep roots in the very foundations of the North American culture.

Of course, I recognize that the whole of humankind is conditioned by deep psychological patterns that produce violence. René Girard and his disciple, the North American Gil Bailie, presented some of the most important sequences in a remarkable manner.[3] They have shown the importance of imitation in the spreading of violence, and omnipresent scapegoating patterns. Western culture as a whole also nurtures some sources of violence of its own: for example, the separation of people from the land is one of the causes of urban violence. The violence coming from the specific characteristics of the French culture does not escape my criticism either. However, my purpose is not to analyze the gigantic question of the roots of violence common to all human beings or to all people of the Western culture; some scholars are working on this difficult study that is of primary importance if humankind wants to avoid being stuck on a dead end road of escalating violence.

My limited purpose here is to gather a series of observations on **what is specific to the birthing of violence in North American culture.** My hypothesis is that some seldom-discussed assumptions within the principles of the U.S. culture foster various violences. As the U.S. culture spreads around the globe, these incriminated principles help generate violence in other parts of the world. If such an hypothesis becomes more and more credible, it means that violence will not stop with political remedies, financial appropriations, or in general organizational decisions. **Only a deep criticism of several principles of the culture can bring light to the situation.** Healing from the current violence will come if and where new principles replace damaging ones. I hope to contribute to envisioning possibilities for transforming a violent culture into a more humane culture of relationships. After each chapter I suggest a few practical questions for reflection.

Some people might be surprised that I, a foreigner, dare take a critical look at the North American culture since it is not fully in my blood. Nevertheless, it is very difficult to be conscious of the true bases of one's own culture. Culture is so much part of one's own being; it secures one's understanding of life and facilitates the management of social relationships. Being critical of one's own culture is often considered sacrilegious or unpatriotic. Only a certain distance from the cultural womb gives a relative freedom. I experienced how some of my friends, returning to the U.S. after months or years in Latin America or Asia, saw their own culture with new eyes; the distance and the immersion into another culture freed them to critique the milk that culturally fed them for so many years. They experienced a true culture shock by encountering anew the culture of their own country. Nurtured by other principles over a period of months or years, they were suddenly asked to participate again in a way of life they questioned and indeed found destructive in many ways. They needed a good debriefing, and some changed their lives radically. Having been born in the French culture, which has its own flaws and sins and having been challenged by various stays in Central and South America, North Africa, Asia and Australia, I am inclined to think that my origin is not a handicap in offering reflections on the North American culture. In fact, my various cultural experiences can add to my ability to appreciate and critique my adopted home.

While a detailed biography is not needed, you might want to know the main experiences and cultural shocks that spawn my reflections.

Born and raised in a family of French bourgeoisie, I shared the pride of my family in the values of the bourgeois sub-culture. That traditional land-owning stratum of society has a high sense of social responsibility. It understood that privileges create duties. Yet, when my Christian faith deepened, I became critical and renounced the blindness of my social class, particularly the dramatic consequences the privileged status of a few has upon the many, even when privilege is tempered by duties well fulfilled. Because of that origin, from early youth I have been in contact with adults in positions of high responsibilities in the industrial, agricultural, business, banking and administrative worlds. The loss of my father when I was two, the start of World War II when I was fifteen, and studies accomplished quickly without difficulties, early challenged and stimulated me to reflect on any experience in a wide context. Members of my family and teachers in elementary grades instilled in me a passion for understanding and reflecting, and equipped me with appropriate methods in order to live out that passion.

Living through four years of Nazi occupation in France gave me an opportunity to reflect on the German culture and its partial rejection of the Nazi sub-culture. Courteous and educated traditional officers of the Werhmacht occupying my grandparents' domain, contrasted with other officers of the S.S. units who believed they had to save the world through Nazism, inflicting violence and showing contempt.

Later a few very special stays in Denmark, Switzerland, and a Basque province of Spain became powerful learning experiences for me. Travels in five other European countries added friendships and data for comparing various aspects of Western European culture.

Two terms of volunteer service in independent Algeria, helping with agricultural reconstruction, gave me a hint into the disastrous consequences of the culture forced by my nation over another nation, even when done "for their own good"! This was an imposition of foreign language, a manner of thinking, and a whole way of life based on values that are not as universal as was believed. In newly independent Algeria I saw a highly developed infrastructure built for exportation of goods or for serving the European minority. For indigenous people struggling with hunger these impressive achievements were useless. That infrastructure (harbors, roads, railroads, irrigation) was in decay. Similarly, their agricultural methods and equipment were inadequate for a country that could not afford expensive import of parts and fertilizers. Frank conversations with Kabyl, Arab, or European friends pointed to the subtle violence of economic interests, and even of well-intentioned initiatives coming from another culture. Local needs were sacrificed to benefit the desire of a colonizing nation.

In addition to these field experiences, I acquired tools for analysis through a variety of academic endeavors. My engineering training at the Institut National Agronomique de Paris, the most noted Institute in France for the study of Sciences and Techniques related to Earth Sciences, required a serious formation in mathematics, biology and physical-chemistry. My ordination as a Roman Catholic priest in France required a solid philosophical and theological training, and I was fortunate to have professors who were not relics from the Middle Ages. I am grateful to all my teachers, in both scientific and religious disciplines, who did not require an accumulation of data and an encyclopedic knowledge, but who taught us how to analyze, to reflect and to build a method adapted to each new problem. They taught us to face life as it is and be ready to help humankind. They provided an important help to my natural curiosity and eagerness to understand.

Valuable experiences enhanced my academic background. As head of the ministry of a prestigious scientific university campus, during six years I developed faithful friendships that continue to this day, almost forty years later. For six more years I worked in a notable architect-urban planner's office. This architect frequently wrote on the social consequences directly related to building lodgings and organizing cities. In these two different responsibilities I learned to listen, to understand, to analyze, to confront ideas and challenge people.

Later, I joined a community in Chicago. It was in a small multiethnic ghetto with a skid row where the rejected sank if they stayed more than a few weeks. Living among Native Americans, Blacks, former coal miners from Appalachia, Latin Americans, Asians, and others, I discovered another aspect of America, the tarnished side of a shining coin. For six years I lived with these rejected people, working as a **day laborer.** Daily, at 5:30 a.m. I arrived at a hiring office and if hired, worked until night at industrial jobs for the minimum wage. No one else wanted these jobs: they were too hard, too dirty, too boring, or too dangerous. In the midst of my companions, without proselytizing I prayed and attempted to be a pleasant co-worker. I worked mainly in metal product factories, sweeping floors (I did it so well that I was offered promotion into the superior category of sweepers!), loading trucks, packing, helping or running punch presses machines and the like. Whatever the job, more than anything I shared the scorn shown to my companion day laborers, bearing inside myself the wound of many injustices inflicted to vulnerable workers. I related these experiences with my religious vocation.

After six years in the Midwest, I lived in Oakland, California for ten years. There I discovered the California style of the

North American culture. I did not soak in every California sub-culture, in particular not in the Marin County very special context; however, I had many opportunities to reflect upon the dynamism of freedom in California. On the other side, either working in a factory or accompanying people struggling for justice, I reflected on persons left outside the dynamic society. I worked for a few years in a small factory, welding lamp shade frames for an employer so tight that extremely qualified workers, with ten to forty years of seniority were paid slightly above the minimum wage. My dilapidated neighborhood was a reminder that California is home not only to movie stars, oil magnates, and lucky gold seekers, but the dispossessed also. The ugly face of poverty is visible to all who choose to see.

While in California I had the privilege of volunteering with Peace Brigades International (PBI) in Guatemala during several stays totaling fifteen months. Our mission was to decrease the injustice of an extremely repressive society run by a military dictator and to help resolve the conflicts in a humane manner. We needed to adapt previous experiences of nonviolent interposition to that specific situation. It was an invaluable challenge. Our most successful method was to accompany endangered people in order to dissuade the death squads from killing them.[4] It was a powerful and sometimes dramatic experience. The Mayan Indians there taught me much! My previous readings became reality as I encountered people who had witnessed incredible violence against themselves and their families. Their sufferings were sometimes the latest phase of a five-hundred-year-old effort to force their communities into the Spanish culture. At other times their sufferings were clearly the result of a market culture seeping in from El Norte. I am grateful for the gifts I received in Guatemala and in other Latin American countries, that is, a wide range of thoughts and data gathered from reflecting with groups on their lives in light of the nonviolent message of the Gospel. Mexico, El Salvador, Panama, Costa Rica, and five South American countries, each one within a special context, showed me their common cultural trends and the obvious differences between each nation.

After my experience in an attractive California, I moved to Las Vegas where a new brand of the American culture was and is in the making. The gambling "industry" works hard and successfully to be seen as an innocuous gaming activity; an indispensable part, they say, of the commercial entertainment needed in a very stressful society. Gambling, proclaim the casino owners, is part of the American Way of Life. In the midst of this new culture, where fake and glitter triumph, I maintained close contacts and friendships with the Native American Shoshone of Nevada, struggling to recover contact with Mother Earth. They introduced me to aspects of the very ancient culture they want to keep. Some Shoshone, conscious of their responsibility towards humankind, try to keep their way of life rooted in the land and in obedience to life and creation's elements.

While in Nevada I accepted shorter responsibilities for Peace Brigades International in Sri Lanka, Haiti, and in North Eastern Quebec with the Innu Indians. All offered exceptional opportunities to encounter people knowledgeable about the local culture—scholars, politicians, diplomats and humble guardians of threatened minorities. I confronted various types of violence and reflected with my companions on how to save a few lives and to help remove groups or nations from the escalating violence.

These have been among the most important opportunities in my life; they, assisted by my scientific, philosophical and theological trainings, served to satisfy my thirst to understand people and their lives. Adding to the learnings during five previous decades, the past twenty-five years in the United States have been very rich in lessons!

The divine presence in the world, especially in that marvelous creature, the human being, is the deepest of all my certitudes. I am an ordained Roman Catholic priest. I belong to a religious Order founded by Saint Francis of Assisi, an amazing Italian who has shown reverence for every creature. I hope that nothing in this writing will offend those who do not share this faith in Jesus Christ, who I believe to be the alpha and omega of Creation.

* * * * *

As I reflect upon all these data and experiences, I do not pretend to present the ultimate (!) thinking on the drama of violence in the North American culture. Readers from the academic community should remember that my aim is not to make a scholarly analysis. Some connections suggested in this writing may nevertheless stimulate their research. It is my deep hope, at the same time, to bring a little light to those who are overwhelmed, sometimes discouraged, but who continue to long and work for an American Way of Life more nurturing and less destructive. All are invited to examine whether their own experiences lead them to resonate with my observations.

All along in this text I hope to show that my hypothesis that some principles of the U.S. culture foster various violences is a daily reality. That does not mean that I do not see the positive and constructive aspects of the U.S. culture which are often described and celebrated. Entrepreneurial spirit, ethics of authenticity, and what is still alive of the

Founding Fathers' understanding of "freedom" are precious elements for any change. Activists and scholars should not forget this richness when speaking of process for change. My purpose does not include that phase. In the Afterword, I present a few notes suggesting some of the possibilities of nonviolence for transformation of the culture. Obviously, this is not a thorough study of pedagogy or strategy for such transformation. That important task remains to be done. Hopefully the action of the General Assembly of the United Nations declaring the years 2000–2010 a Decade for a Culture of Peace and Nonviolence will stimulate such studies on pedagogy, encouraged by the UNESCO aim of educating for a peace based on nonviolence.

I hope the critical statements that I offer to my American friends will not hurt their national pride. Whatever culture gave us the security of our first years, it is difficult to hear critiques. People become more defensive than they are willing to recognize. However, an adult needs to denounce any false security. A mature person accepts the critique of one's cultural bases in order to seek remedies. Being able to do so should be one's pride. May my love for the United States and for Americans help in their critical look at their culture in order to remedy violence.

CHAPTER ONE

What Do We Mean by Violence, Nonviolence, Culture, Market Culture, and Principles?

T HE FOLLOWING TEXT will frequently include the words *violence, nonviolence, culture, market culture and principles*. In this writing they are used with a relatively precise meaning, expressed in this chapter. I will also present a tentative definition of *market culture*, a rather new expression.

Violence

Even though this writing is not a treatise on *violence*, the overuse of this word necessitates clarity on how it will be used in this text. Here the word *violence* will be reserved to **situations and actions originating with humans or human structures coupled with foreseeable physical, moral or economic harm, degradation, death or destruction to humans, or creation.** This definition shows clearly that violence is not only the physical aggression that most people have in mind when they speak of violent acts— street aggressions, rape, terrorist bombs, revolution, or the cruel civil war. The Oxford Universal Dictionary defined *violence* as "exertion of any physical force as to inflict injury or damage to persons or property." Violence is every action or inaction of persons or structures insensitive to and oppressive of the dignity, the values and the rights of human persons or other creatures. It negates the fundamental humanness or sacredness of the person or the creature. Violence can be the result of psychological, moral, cultural, or even spiritual forces.

Structural violence can come from an institution, an organization, or a mechanism. More frequently than it is realized, it can come from a cultural pattern or way of thinking. In fact, most structural violences are rooted in ways of thinking, especially when they are hidden underneath a so-called "order" or dismissed as something obvious. Sometimes smiling and softly spoken violences serve dehumanizing structures. The degradation can happen by denying to others minimum psychological, economic, cultural, or spiritual needs, as it is observed towards those who become homeless.

I will never use the word violence to describe the destructive power of natural phenomena such as earthquakes, floods, or tornadoes. The media's use of the word *violence* in these natural catastrophes is inappropriate. It would be better to speak of the *destructive power* of a tornado. A tornado is not violent, even though it can be tremendously destructive.

Some people speak of the violence between animals. This disputable topic will not be part of the following reflections. In this text *violence* refers to that which comes from human beings and human organizations or structures.

Violence is often confused with strength, aggressiveness, combativeness, and assertiveness, to mention only a few sibling realities. *Strength*, which has a power to initiate, is also a power to resist a force or attack. Strength as resistance is needed for any personal, social or cultural change. *Aggressiveness* is related to the need for self-affirmation and is a manifestation of vitality and strength. Passive people, who constitute the most impressive majority, need often to have their aggressiveness awakened to start a struggle. *Aggressivity,* often considered synonymous of aggressiveness, sometimes brings a note of antipathy, disrespect, cruelty, and hate, all feelings that should be controlled if a human being is to become an adult. *Combativeness* is a set of fixed qualities of character enabling one to fight against, contend, or oppose vigorously. *Assertiveness* is the ability to state or express positively, to defend or maintain. Assertiveness suggests self-confidence, especially in the expression of an opinion.

One further distinction that is necessary for our reflection is the difference between violence and conflict. People often equate conflict with violence. Some parents or educators have even developed this confusion and encourage youth to avoid conflicts. They do so either when they lack methods of resolving conflicts or because they are afraid an open conflict will change the status quo. Sadly, the Gospel has often been misunderstood on this point. Loving one another and loving your enemies does not mean doing so without conflict. In fact, this Gospel misunderstanding was the basis of the Marxist critique of Christianity. Karl Marx saw that the use of the Gospel to avoid conflict was an opium. He invited the intensification of the conflict in order to mobilize energy for social change. Similarly, Germany's National Socialism praised a so-called "beneficial violence" in order to avoid apathy of the masses. Without going into these excesses, we should accept the fact that conflicts are a reality of life. No human life exists without a weaving of conflicts, as interests differ, points of view vary, and fear or anger inflates difficulties or oppositions.

The constructive purpose of a conflict is to establish justice between adversaries. People who have been traumatized by unsuccessful conflicts should revise their judgment and accept the fact that conflicts are needed to enter into a world of communion. Violence is a dysfunction in conflict resolution. An adversary who uses means that threaten the humanness or the life of the opponent reveals a desire for murder, whether partial or total, symbolic or real. There resides the dysfunction in the conflict. Nonviolence addresses that specific problem and seeks the mutual healing of the parties in conflict.

Nonviolence

A concise definition of nonviolence is difficult to arrive at, but what was said above about violence gives some parameters for understanding *nonviolence*. Nonviolence is more than the refusal of violent means. **It is a method for resolving conflicts and injustices, and it is a spirit.** Various conceptions of nonviolence exist, but most groups who call themselves nonviolent refer to great figures such as Jesus Christ, Gandhi, Martin Luther King Jr., Aung San Suu Kyi, César Chavez or the Mothers of the Plaza de Mayo in Argentina. That is the vision of nonviolence used in this text.

Nonviolence is the "force" or the "witness of truth." Truth is not only what moralists call truth—a statement conforming to the reality; it is also the fact that human beings in their core are longing for living relationships and communion, and for experiencing a life consistent with that yearning. Nonviolence can be either spontaneous or organized. Some people who do not know the theory or practice of Mahatma Gandhi's systematized active nonviolence spontaneously use the same basic behavior and method. They refuse to answer violence by physical, verbal, or psychological violence. Instead they seek to establish a new balance of power by disarming their opponent with the inner power arising from their liberty, courage, steadfastness, or love. Some spontaneous nonviolent behaviors show the amazing creativity of courageous, loving persons free from fear and inhabited by an uncommon strength.

The same opposition to violence enfleshing an inner strength and a true freedom is what Mahatma Gandhi placed at the base of his "satyagraha" campaigns. To the spontaneous acts he added the power of the number of people involved, as well as the need for time and a well thought out strategy. These last factors are keys in creating a new balance of power. The opponents may be touched by the behavior of the oppressed who refuse to retaliate and instead show their willingness to suffer rather than to impose a suffering on others. It might awaken in them a longing for such courage and love in order to become free from violence and hate. Such a result happens only in the best of cases. Experienced nonviolent practitioners realize that seldom, if ever, will the power of love instantaneously disarm their adversary. If such a change does not occur, then a strategy should be deployed to exert constraint so that the opponent feels compelled, in his own interest or in the interest of the structure of violence that he serves, to accept the just demand of his adversary. In both processes respect for the adversary's sacredness is a fundamental element of the nonviolent pressure. Most likely it will need to be exerted over a long period of time and with a large number of people.

From the above reflections we see how the efficiency of active nonviolence requires that activists believe in a common humanness that they share with their adversaries. Whether religious or secular terminology is used, it is necessary to recognize a common inner reality acting inside the human beings; the believers name it the divine presence. Nonviolent practitioners are requested to have confidence in the intrinsic goodness of every human being, the opponent as well as themselves. Nonviolent methodology for conflict resolution requires the recognition of the unity of humankind and, as a consequence, the dignity of all, even the servants of injustice. Nonviolence requires great strength, and patience. The nonviolent person witnesses a fundamental truth: The human being is neither all bad nor all good. The nonviolent person is not a doormat or a slug. Some people describe nonviolent action as an integral struggle. Its objective is simultaneously to eradicate injustice and to transform both the perpetrators and the victims of injustice. The French author Olivier Lacombe calls it "the civil reclaiming of truth." This is very different from what some people call pragmatic or tactical nonviolence which is concerned only about results and does not require humanistic or religious convictions.

If not otherwise mentioned, *"nonviolence" will mean the active nonviolence that aims at the eradication of violences and the birthing of a new type of resolution for the tensions and conflicts that create violences and injustices.*[5] Spontaneous nonviolence, humanistic or religious, is important, but the Gandhian active nonviolence offers, for opposing violence, a coherent tool which by its clearly marked phases can be adapted to the most complex situations. Its main lines are precise. The Jainist religious tradition in which Gandhi grew up, and the Gospel that touched him deeply, allied their richness to give the spirit to this methodology.

An aspect of the nonviolent strategy is the active *"non-collaboration"* with injustice; it intends to paralyze the adversary or the adverse system but respects the opponent. Martin

Luther King often called this active non collaboration "*non-violent resistance*." The nonviolent person reveres the opponent and respects her or his physical well-being and dignity. This allows the opponent to realize the damage he is doing. This non-collaboration with injustice is very different from the "*passive resistance*" to injustice, which lacks full respect for the dignity of the opponent, and even sometimes coexists with resentment and hate. This passive resistance, highly criticized by M.K. Gandhi,[6] can sometimes redress an injustice or violence, but it is far from the nonviolent process.

M.L. King enumerated the following six principles of nonviolence presented here in a shorter form. First, nonviolent resistance is not a method for cowards; it does resist. If one uses this method because one is afraid or merely lacks the instruments of violence, that person is not truly nonviolent. Second, nonviolence does not seek to defeat or humiliate the opponent, but to win his friendship and understanding. The aftermath of nonviolence is the creation of the beloved community, while the aftermath of violence is tragic bitterness. Third, the nonviolent attack is directed against forces of evil rather than against persons who happen to be doing the evil. It is evil that the nonviolent resister seeks to defeat, not the persons perpetrating the evil. Fourth, nonviolent resistance is a willingness to accept suffering without striking back. Suffering, the nonviolent resister realizes, has tremendous educational and transforming possibilities. Fifth, nonviolent resistance avoids not only external physical violence but also internal violence of the spirit. The nonviolent resister not only refuses to shoot the opponent but also refuses to hate her or him. Sixth, nonviolent resistance is based on the conviction that the universe is on the side of justice. Consequently, the believer in nonviolence has deep faith in the future. Whether we call it an unconscious process, an impersonal Brahman, or a Personal Being of matchless power and infinite love, a creative force in this universe works to bring the disconnected aspects of reality into a harmonious whole.[7]

Culture

In this text the word culture means *Way of Life*. In order to avoid ambiguity let us remember some other common uses of the word. In a general sense a person who has developed a critical perspective of reality, sound judgment, and discriminating taste is deemed a person of culture. Many people also use the words culture and cultural in reference to the literature, the arts, and the manners of a people. Some countries have Cultural Centers where arts and crafts are developed and where knowledge is acquired without previous academic background. In these places new cultural expressions of a generation can be tested. Any promotional effort of tourism in an area includes the list of cultural events such as concerts, theater plays, poetry readings, art exhibitions, and historical or archeological displays. Both expressions of the previous centuries and of the present time are on the program.

Many countries have an administration to take care of the cultural heritage in order to avoid the destruction or alienation of past or present treasures. UNESCO actively promotes and funds this concern, as some treasures of the past are really a patrimony of the whole human race. When people refer to lost civilizations, generally their understanding of culture is one of "a particular form or stage of civilization, as that of a certain nation or period." The various writings, paintings, sculptures, and architectures witness the life and preoccupations of past human groups. The Greek culture, the aboriginal culture, the Eskimo culture, the Inca culture, and others stimulate numerous studies.

Moving from the traditional presentation of the Museums, and using the new knowledge of sociology, the *Musée de l'Homme* in Paris and the *Museo de Antropología* in Mexico City expanded such a narrow comprehension of culture and sought to understand what was the real life of these disappeared human beings; they presented their way of life in day to day activities. The culture is then understood as "the whole of social structures, religious and art expressions, which differentiates a group from another." These two museums, now followed by a few others, invite us to interpret archeological and historical discoveries in order to understand what our forebears or our remote cousins valued, thought, felt, and did.

This comes close to the contemporary understanding of what is meant by a *Way of Life*. In this writing the word *culture* will be used in this context. "Culture is the whole way of life, material, intellectual and spiritual, of a given society."[8] To that definition this text includes the added qualifications "transmitted from one generation to another, and differentiating one group from another." **Reference to North American culture here means the American Way of Life, which identifies the people living in the United States, and has been transmitted by previous generations.**

Inside the continental United States various cultures exist simultaneously. The American Way of Life, however, represents the dominant culture led by the Anglo-Saxon component of the nation. At the same time, inside the U.S. other cultures exist: the most noticeable are the Afro-American, the Hispanic, and the Native cultures. When ethnic neighborhoods existed in North American cities, other cultures from Europe or Asia were quite alive and identifiable.

Market Culture

The expression *market culture* is relatively new. During the last few years I advanced this wording to describe accurately the U.S. situation.[9] Because of the American economic leadership, this expression also describes the situation in a growing number of countries. *Market culture* will be used to mean **the culture born from the womb of the market.** A following chapter will develop this notion. For now this shorter definition will suffice. A market culture is **a culture in which the laws of the market economy take the place of the principles on which previous cultures had been established.** It is not at all the marketing of cultural goods—books, films, paintings, etc.—as some people might be tempted to interpret the expression.

Market culture should not be confused with the most well-known realities of market economy, marketing, market place, and consumption. Surely there are relationships among all of these, but the market culture is clearly a culture in which economic rationalism takes the place of previous principles, which had their roots in morals or religions. Economic rationalism presents the free market mechanisms as inescapable. It assumes that these mechanisms are part of the laws of the universe, as the law of gravity or the principles of thermodynamics.[10] This gives them a divine prestige, and sustains their claim to the right of being foundations of an understanding and praxis of human life.

The main difficulty in explaining and giving a short definition of market culture is that the same words are used by the disappearing culture and the new market culture, but not with the same meaning. Many people believe the North American culture still rests on the established principles valued by the forefathers of the country. A substitution of meaning has happened subtly, as during a sleep. The points of reference have changed. Market culture has established new points of reference in every area of our lives.

Principles

Frequently I will use the expression "principles of the culture", when speaking of human based cultures, of the market culture, or of that special human based culture which is the nonviolent culture.

The word principle will be understood not only as the ultimate source of the culture, or a motivating force inside the culture, but what gives a foundation to what is happening now. In this book a principle is the reality which makes that which is happening now inevitable. The consequences of cultural principles are wider than what is recognized at first.

CHAPTER TWO

Why Were So Many Wonderful Possibilities Not Realized?

THE INTRODUCTION TO THIS BOOK posed the question of why so many possibilities of the North American make-up, "so many wonderful promises, so many hopes, wither or even vanish away." I will now present some examples of promises that had given me hope and then did not bear the expected fruit.

In 1989 I asked a musician and song composer which contemporary promising singers convey values that challenge the prevalent way of life. He named a few, then added, "these were promising, but have been co-opted by the dominant culture. The most recent non-co-opted figure was Joan Baez in her struggle against the Vietnam War. She gave hope to many, but I do not know anyone more recent." This opinion seems valid today.

The events of 1968 and the hippie sub-culture fired up people of various ages and backgrounds, and I was one of them. The best of the hippie reactions would be beneficial to the whole Western culture, following a renewal in the U.S. Our community in Chicago had close relationships with many small communities built on hippies' intuitions, especially that humanness and individuality should not be subordinated to money or organization. Progressively these communities vanished. When it became clear that very little changed in the foundations of the American Way of Life, all those who had been lifted up by hope became dismayed. The hippies and their friends revolted against being considered objects, but the establishment and the prevalent principles realized a subtle dismantling of the revived realities and allowed only a few nostalgic thoughts to survive.

In a similar way during the last few decades, I followed with amazement how in this country saving the earth and humankind from pollution and destruction became a growing concern, and a significant sign of hope in a future. From school children to university students, from small villages to huge cities, concern developed amazingly. In reading carefully the business pages of the newspapers, I soon noticed the money makers attention to the incredible dynamism of the ecological movement.[11] They saw a good opportunity for their enrichment in using the ecological vocabulary for new profits. Almost every corporation developed a public relations strategy to persuade us of their genuine concern for the environment. While some may be sincere and efficient, how many corporations even repaired the disastrous consequences of their own previous actions?

Other hopeful initiatives directed their efforts towards the destructive consequences of individualism that sociologists, politicians and moralists have denounced. They saw an important priority in building a new community based social fabric. Concerned people created groups, organizations, new regulations or education in a community spirit, and later saw new forms of individualism growing inside these new community structures. Many causes nurture individualism, but interestingly a study has shown how in the U.S. the decline of associations, neighborhood and interest groups, happened during eight years of the fifties. This decrease followed the number of families owning a television set, which increased from 10% to 90% during the same period.[12] Those working to develop a communitarian spirit and communitarian patterns should take into account that their efforts are simultaneously countered by the merchants controlling the television channels who encourage passivity and individualistic patterns of behavior. Alluring potential consumers when they are alone and vulnerable to any offer or temptation is a key marketing ploy. Who of us has not been a victim of such a tactic? Weakened by our loneliness, we bought something that we would never have acquired if friends or family members had been with us. Even though sometimes such companions may encourage the buying, more often they expose the advertising fallacy or encourage resistance to a convincing salesperson. Television viewing is a requisite of the American Way of Life; any TV advertising is certain of an impact. Local newspapers often do not announce upcoming events if they have been publicized by the TV.

On the international scene, I followed with great interest how a majority of the global population placed their hopes in the 1992 Rio de Janeiro U.N. Conference on Environment and Development. They were frustrated by corporations' pressure upon the U.S. representatives, who obediently refused to sign the most important agreements, thus placing the U.S.A. in an isolated position. The Kyoto conference on global warming in December 1997, has shown the same ecological choices of the U.S.A. being dictated by corporate interests and not by the future of the planet.

How sad it is to see the withering of so many wonderful promises. What a waste! Bitterness or despair takes the place of reasonable hope. During my twenty-five years in this country, that dramatic loss brought me deep pain. I have seen many generous, gifted, creative, energetic people, eventually align themselves with the prevalent and destructive behavior of the culture we live in.

Not all the cases of aborted potentialities are related to the culture. In this country, as in other parts of the world, people who lack perseverance are discouraged because results are not immediately visible. Everywhere, people who have not yet found their true self are especially vulnerable; they have difficulty focusing. However, individual weakness in character and interiority does not explain all the cases. The ambient mentality and the domination of structures that impose their mechanisms on new initiatives shortly after their birth are the most likely explanations. The challenge to old patterns and the creation of new cultural elements have not been accepted by the dominant culture that continues, nevertheless, to proclaim that the North American culture is a melting pot that welcomes various values and behaviors.

The history of nuclear weapons offers another dramatic example of cultural structures generating more violence and giving short life to any new sign of hope. For many years the U.S. tested nuclear weapons in the Pacific Islands, and after 1951 in Nevada sixty miles North of Las Vegas. For years many of my friends struggled against the nuclear testings, and I participated with them at a large number of demonstrations. Even before their use, nuclear weapons have damaging effects on health and environment. When they were used on Hiroshima and Nagasaki and at various nuclear test sites, the human toll grew dramatically and ecological consequences appeared. The down-winders of eastern Nevada and southern Utah suffer high rates of cancer and death. Health concerns became the reason for closing the Semipalatinsk test site in Kazakhstan, then part of the U.S.S.R. I heard well-informed specialists from Western and Soviet camps assert how mining, ore processing, manufacturing and nuclear waste storage and testing damaged millions of people for life. Many of them are now dead.[13] As a first step against nuclear weapons production and plans for their use, a few organized groups struggled to stop nuclear testing, often proclaimed by the government as indispensable. Nevada Desert Experience, American Peace Test, Greenpeace, Healing Global Wounds and Shundahai Network, have all worked hard over the years to end testing. At the gate of the Nevada Test Site, they organized prayers, vigils, demonstrations, nonviolent actions of civil disobedience and blockades in order to mobilize more people against the testings. Throughout the country places of technological research, manufacturing and stockpiling of nuclear weapons became objects of protest and of various creative actions. In Washington D.C., New York City and Geneva other organizations lobbied decision makers to cease the nuclear testings. Opposition to nuclear testing and nuclear weapons grew as information circulated regarding their past and present damages. People who had thought the nuclear madness was inevitable began to hope for a better future.

As soon as a moratorium on the nuclear testings was announced in 1992, it became clear that stopping the tests does not end the mentality that started them. It eliminates neither the financial nor the industrial structures serving the nuclear weapons industry. When treaties limiting the number of nuclear weapons were accepted, the builders of nuclear weapons obtained contracts for dismantling them. Later, the contractors fought against signing of the Comprehensive Test Ban Treaty (C.T.B.T.) of September 1996 that they considered catastrophic because signing countries committed themselves to work towards the elimination of nuclear weapons. This reaction of financial interests was not surprising. However, a sizable group of generals, including retired Air Force General George Lee Butler, a former commander in chief of the Strategic Air Command, said publicly that "nuclear weapons are inherently dangerous, hugely expensive, militarily inefficient and morally indefensible." [14] Still, some voices continue to proclaim that the Comprehensive Test Ban Treaty should not impede other methods of testing in order to build **new nuclear weapons!** In 1997, two new subcritical tests[15] were undertaken at the Nevada Test Site. In September 1997 President Clinton himself wrote to the senate describing his policy to "ensure the continued application of our human scientific resources to those programs on which continued progress in nuclear technology depends."[16] Any doubt vanished about the U.S. policy against the treaty requirement to eliminate nuclear weapons. Hope was destroyed.

One should not be misled into believing that the nuclear policy results from the powerful few militaristic people, the hawks. Nuclear weapons are a manifestation of a deeper reality ingrained in the whole life and culture of the country: the need for total supremacy. Sharing the general feeling of their fellow citizens, some of my best activist friends find it hard and dramatic to recognize the mere existence of this fact: this country feels the need for a military power that cannot be challenged by anyone else. The governments can change, the politicians can vary their policies, but as long as the principles guiding the culture stay the same, as long as the general mentality of the majority does not change, **the decisions will not change.**[17] During election campaigns I heard my friends proclaiming that their candidate can change various previous policies. Shortly after, despair and cynicism followed. The media are in the hands of a few powerful corporations, and their influence on public opinion is well documented. The Gulf War demonstrated this principle of total superiority orchestrated by the media. This principle of U.S. policy has deep connections with the **Number One Syndrome** explored further in another chapter. No objective reflection on the world resources, the poverty of billions of human beings, and the ecological catastrophe in progress has so far decreased the strength of **the need for total supremacy. It is a principle of the culture.** Never mind if the use of nuclear weapons jeopardizes the survival of both adversaries! Xenophobia and the arrogant display of sophisticated, deadly weapons are so ingrained that the obvious destructive consequences of such behavior fail to deter the drive for supremacy. Mass destruction in order to keep power, or at least to annihilate a potential enemy, will then bring our own death along with the death of the enemy.

The signing of the C.T.B.T. did not remove the Damocles' sword hanging over humankind for so many years. The nuclear clock was turned backward only a few minutes.[18] Cultural patterns inside the U.S.A. overcame the potential benefits of an international mobilization towards elimination of nuclear weapons. Hope was alive, but the culture overwhelmed it even though it might not be a final triumph.

The relations between the dominant Anglo-American culture and the Hispanic and Native-American cultures is another striking example of aborted possibilities. My contacts with Hispanic and Native American cultures kept alive in me the hope that they would bring beneficial changes in the White-Anglo-Saxon-Protestant culture. This same hope is held by many Americans conscious of the drifting of their culture. These minorities' cultures could help rebuild a communitarian spirit, give strength to family ties, challenge the work ethic, rebuild respect for the land, or bring a stronger sense of celebration as is naturally expressed in Hispanic fiestas. The reality is that Indians out of the reservations or third generation Hispanics are frequently so completely assimilated by the prevalent culture that their original richness has faded. No wonder minorities often speak of the Anglo-Saxon culture as the dominant culture. Assimilations of minorities carried out under the guise of national unity represent a terrible loss for the American people. The richness brought by the various immigrants has been sacrificed to a narrow national uniformity. Similar behavior was observed with Asians in the first part of the 20th century. Now the large number of immigrants from Mexico spreads all over the country the fear of a disequilibrium in the cultural identity of the U.S.A. This fear and all the previous factors have led to the physical expulsion of humble carriers of many beneficial values for the nation. These reactions may be common to every majority culture in a nation. A sizable minority of North Americans expresses shock at finding these patterns inside an immigrant country where the message of the Statue of Liberty still resounds.

Is there even a widespread desire to learn from the cultures of new immigrants? The remarkable effort during the last twenty years by various Christian communities to provide sanctuary for Central Americans threatened in their homeland might bear some fruit with time. Some affluent people began to learn from the materially poor. North American parishes linked with parishes of Third World countries favored exchange of persons and understanding of other ways of life. Hopefully this "reverse mission" and the preferential option for the poor will also develop inside the U.S.A. a desire to learn from economically poor countries whose culture is often looked down upon. Arrogance may not be here for ever.

Australia, which has not respected the aboriginal culture, nevertheless has been more attentive to recognize the rich variety of her immigrants. In the U.S., what rich cultural elements were Italian immigrants able to give to the country and the culture that received them? Although their entrepreneurial qualities have been recognized, their input into the American Way of Life seems limited to pizza, spaghetti and the Mafia. At least that is what I observed! Where did their amazing sense of beauty go? I do not see it anyplace. Promises brought by new blood have been annihilated by the principles of the dominant culture. The open mind of many North American individuals did not prevail over cultural structures in which they live.

Persons who feel overwhelmed told me not to burden them more by any reflection on negative aspects of their own culture. An only negative way of looking at the world is not healthy. However, a refusal to look at cultural flaws and defects is likewise unhealthy. The inability to face unpleasant realities may be a sign of psychological depression. The nation of the United States with all its richness deserves better than this fearful attitude.

It is my confidence in the American people that challenges me to offer my observations and reflections to my American friends. The previous examples are presented to help readers to discover for themselves what their realistic hopes were which did not bear fruits. Is it only circumstantial events that provoke the failure? Or is the destruction created by some undiscussed principles operative in the culture? Looking at these frustrated hopes, we need to keep in mind the purpose of these reflections: to motivate people for a change that can heal the main sources of cultural violence.

Questions for Reflection

- *Remember situations that offered you a serious hope for a profound change in society or culture.*

  Did you hope for a change inside the dominant mentality? Or was it for a change of structures? A new law? The creation of a new organization?

  Was it related to politics? Domestic policy? Or foreign policy? Was it brought up by music? Plastic arts? Literature? By a scientific discovery? Or a technological progress?

- *What made this hope vanish?*

  Was it an unrealistic hope? Had the data not been well analyzed? Were enemy forces openly fighting against it?

  Did you observe a fatigue in those who were working for the change?

  Did you observe some prevalent ways of thinking or doing that transformed the direction of the change or twisted its meaning?

  All in all, would you attribute the failure of the promises to the actors of the change or to the swallowing up by the prevalent culture?

- *What were your reactions when you discovered the withering of these promises? What were the reactions of people around you?*

CHAPTER THREE

Market Culture:
Its Emergence and Effects

Violences Coming from the Market World.
Where Is the Human Being?

EVEN WHEN THE GUNS AND BOMBS are silent all over the world, newspapers and television daily pour into me the latest news of a gigantic economic war. Is it because my reading of the newspaper starts with the business pages? I do not think so. Violence in many forms comes from the market world and is presented as the normal result of progress. War produces casualties, and one should not be surprised that the weakest country or corporation suffers from the most powerful, say the cold blooded strategists of the business world. Hostile corporate take overs, speculation, unbalanced international trade are daily news, but the resulting violence does not shock people as much as the violence of wars and terrorist acts.

Frequently too, my social worker friends lament that advertising increases consumption, thus creating new wants and even new needs. They mention shopping fever, addiction to consumption, credit debt leading many to dead end situations. Helpless, they witness family destruction and sufferings which are not natural fatalities and are caused by artificial needs. Lately, a group started a clever campaign against what they called an outbreak of **affluenza.** They present two meanings of that new epidemic: "1- The bloated, sluggish and unfulfilled feeling resulting from trying to buy all the latest stuff and keep up with the Joneses. 2- An unsustainable addiction to consumption and economic growth without regard for the consequences to our families, communities or the environment."[19] Other groups and recent books point out the same disease of our society.[20] Aspects of consumerism and of the market bring indisputable advantages for some, but at the same time terrible destruction for many. Debts piling up, overwork, fractured families, and stress are the most obvious damages. It is universally recognized that economic warfare and consumption problems cause countless violences. Nevertheless, my focus here is not on these events but on a more dramatic fact: new cultural principles coming from the market functioning have replaced former cultural principles. We now live in a market **culture.** This market culture is bigger than, but includes, consumption and economic battles for control of the market, both of which are often understood as the source of many ills. More deeply than consumerism, market culture penetrates the whole social fabric, and the consequences of this penetration are powerful, subtle, and destructive.

The critique of the market culture is **not** a critique of the market economy or of the market society. The criticisms addressed to the market culture are related to the substitution of moral principles by principles that had been established for the material success of the market system.

When I think of the market culture, I reflect on my experience. I read or hear about factory closures in one North American town after another. Serving coffee or soup at the line organized by the Catholic Worker in Las Vegas I often encounter professional workers whose factory closed. Jobless, penniless and evicted, they arrive in Las Vegas in their over-loaded car with their partner and children, hoping that in the nation's fastest growing city they will find a job. In reality most stay homeless at least a few months. During twenty-five years I have encountered both decision makers and victims of factory closures. Corporations cite competition and impend-ing bankruptcy as the rationale for relocating factories to places where cheaper labor is available, in Asia or Latin America. The management and the board invoke the laws of the market. They speak of survival, but are interested by a larger profit. Workers are rarely consulted, and if they are, they do not weigh much in the decision. U.S. workers who have been faithful to their employer for decades are left without possible employment in their area. Family dramas, suicides, poverty, say the corporations, cannot be considered. Competition cannot listen to calls for compassion. Market laws should be obeyed, proclaim the boards, formed of men and women who otherwise can be sensitive. The workers know that such an economic rationalism is flawed. People are not objects. They are human beings who collaborate through their muscles and brains to provide for their families. Peti-tions, strikes, demonstrations and solidarity expressed by fellow workers fail to reverse the decision. The workers lose the fight. It is the law of the market!

The law of the market touches every facet of North American society, even the health care system. A friend in severe pain from a stone in the bile duct is rushed to a hospital that refuses to take him because he has no insurance. Finally he lands in the emergency room of a county hospital where he waits fifteen hours, with slight relief from painkillers, before being treated. This case, which is not isolated, shows how market considerations operative in the health and insurance systems prevail over concern for the illness and life-threatening pain of a human being. Life, human dignity, confidentiality, respect for family and the needs of children become subservient to economic laws. The most sacred realities of life are no longer considered. "You have to be realistic," proclaim the managers, "we live in a tough competitive society."

The political rhetoric presents the U.S.A. as compassionate, a country giving food aid to the poor of the world. How do the previous examples fit with such a statement? Good intentions and compassionate feelings might be real, but the structure of thinking and the organization of the economy impose inhuman decisions in the name of the sacrosanct competition.

Consider the example of Mexico. Changes in Mexican laws were a condition requested for the signing of North American Free Trade Agreement (N.A.F.T.A.). Land distribution written in the Mexican Constitution of 1917 as a result of the "Revolution" should be terminated. In Chiapas the land reform had never been completed. Consequently, landless people experienced open violence when it was announced that land distribution was canceled and the sale of the plots received after the "Revolution"[21] was authorized allowing outsiders to buy them. The Zapatista revolt in Chiapas started January 1, 1994, the same day N.A.F.T.A. became effective. The insurrectionist Zapatistas assert that "N.A.F.T.A. is a death sentence for the Indians."[22]

Politicians and the North American media continue to present N.A.F.T.A. as the American parallel to the European Common Market. I saw the birth and growth of the Common Market and can compare the formation of N.A.F.T.A. with the creation of the European Community. Western European countries may have more common cultural elements than Mexico with the United States, even though many southern and western states had received at first the Hispanic culture. Nevertheless, it is worth noting that as a first step the European Common Market sought to unite people of various countries previously divided by wars—mainly France and Germany—and to encourage exchanges among them, gradually suppressing the borders.[23] In an opposite manner, a stricter filter of the southern U.S. border of the U.S.A. occurred when N.A.F.T.A. started. Improvement in human relationships was not a criterion for accepting N.A.F.T.A.. The interchange of persons and wealth among partner countries is out of its concerns.[24] The unity of all North America is not an objective. The two main motivations for N.A.F.T.A. are economic: to widen the market for North American products, and to discourage Mexican people from emigrating to the U.S., as industrial plants would emerge in their own country.[25] Understandably, every country is concerned about immigration and wants to regiment it. When the U.S., however, limits the entry of Mexicans in order to maintain a privileged status, it violates the most precious principles of the U.S. culture. Opponents to restrictive measures point out that the country was made of immigrants, some of them illegal. They recalled the immensity of the territory and the human resources brought by new adults ready to join the work force. These observations did not convince legislators who established very restrictive laws directed only at the southern members of N.A.F.T.A., which some rhetorical speeches continue to present as the "North American Common Market." Once more the rationale for these new policies are "a market requirement" whose necessity is not debatable.

In another international event the dramatic primacy of the market principles over moral ones was displayed in the

U.S. delegation's votes at the Rio Conference on the Environment in 1992. The majority of the countries and a large
number of U.S. citizens pleaded for international solidarity to
address global threats related to ozone depletion and rain
forest destruction. To safeguard their interests, U.S. corporations trampled these global concerns. The follow up conference in Kyoto in December 1997 was disappointing for the
same reasons.

Another example of the market economy prevailing over
human realities of a Third World country comes from my time
in Guatemala. In 1983, the *de facto* Chief of State of Guatemala, General Rios Montt, developed the *model villages* in
order to remove the Indian population from their traditional
hamlets where they could give some logistical help to the
guerrillas. Regrouped in houses along straight streets easier to
control, they were given a very small field to cultivate. The
strategy of the army, associated with market pressure from
the U.S.A., found an ingenious solution. On their small plot
the villagers would cultivate flowers to sell in Miami, and
then buy needed corn from the U.S.A. This solution, very
logical inside the market economy, did not consider the fact
that corn cultivation is a religious act for Mayas. The corn, a
benevolent god, took care of their survival over many centuries. The market economy's imposing its logic on the local
culture attacked a sacred reality for the Mayas. Their culture,
way of life, relates to corn as a cultivation and as a food, even
if it is more expensive to grow it than to import it. Economic
rationalists cannot understand the Mayas' choice that seems
to them to go backwards!

I could continue to give more examples of what I personally witnessed or of events reported in well informed studies.
The few previous examples show how market principles are
often in conflict with a culture based on human values. These

differences arise from the dignity or humanness of persons requesting respect in the face of corporate decision. Human based values invite a reverence toward the preciousness of every creature whether human or non human.

A new set of values coming from the market's womb has birthed a new culture which we call the **market culture**. Hearing the expression "market culture", many frown and their eyes become inquisitive. They are at a loss. This is not surprising, as a definition of market culture is just emerging. In order to understand what exactly the market culture is and how values have changed, I will offer a brief description of the birth of the market culture; then we will reflect on the exploratory definition given in chapter one. After that I will speak of the violence linked to the emergence and growth of the market culture. Its exclusive concern for profit making has brought a casualness that does not respect the sacredness of every creature and deeply erodes the humanness of many. How did financial interests impose their values of rationalism and material efficiency on a country which had been founded on Christian values and is recently benefiting from the Buddhist caution about wealth?

From Trading Post to Market Culture

Let us follow the beginnings and the evolution of the market. How far back do we need to go into prehistory to encounter the market institution? Archeology reveals that human beings, individually or in groups, started trading very early. Excess of certain items and need for other goods brought into existence barter between neighbors. One did not have grains, but had abundance of fruits. Another, close to a seashore, needed fur from inland dwellers. Still another, after a successful hunt, could give his neighbors meat in exchange for tools, or materials for a new hut, or seeds.

Later, tribes and villages established market-places that still exist in less industrialized areas. Here people come from their huts or their hamlets bringing the excess of their needs and looking for what they do not have: vegetables, fruits, grains, animals, and handicrafts changed hands. These rudimentary and colorful places provided some services and, quite often, some forms of entertainment. When money became more common, exchanges grew easier and bartering gave place to buying and selling. Larger market places were established. More structured civilizations organized caravans carrying fur, wool, salt, spices, silk, or metals over long roads snaking across the continents. With slight differences arising from geography, climate, and cultures, this succession of phases forms the general scheme describing the birth and the first steps of trade.

Centuries later, roads, canals, and progress in carriage and ship-building made possible exchanges among distant areas of the world. Some zones of the globe specialized in specific agriculture or manufacturing, favored by their climate, their resources, or the special gifts of their population. With the accumulation of capital came the rise of industry; exchanges increased again, this time in a gigantic manner. Manufactured goods in one place needed buyers from other areas. Transportation became key to these exchanges and made spectacular progress within a few decades.

The growth of industrialization and its associated accumulation of capital created human struggles and an imbalance resulting from a conflict of values. The profit that entrepreneurs desired conflicted with the basic needs of the workers, their security, the health of children and women, and the respect for family ties. Dramatic struggles followed. Workers and moralists fought for the respect of fundamental human rights. Progressively, painfully, laws and regulations imposed a certain ethic on manufacturing and commerce. For several centuries the various Western societies submitted, at least partially, to a certain economic ethic born from the values they treasured. Most people agreed that the market cannot run wild and should follow moral principles. Moralists, free thinkers, communists, popes, bishops and religious leaders spoke on these topics during the last hundred years, especially after the memorable papal encyclical *Rerum Novarum* in 1891, twenty-four years after Karl Marx harshly critiqued the wild market in *The Capital.*

In the last few decades a radical change occurred that many do not yet comprehend: **Politicians, ordinary people and even ethicists began to bow unquestioningly to the laws of market.** Poverty was presented as the worst evil to fight. As a result, material development became a priority, and the free market pretended to be the most efficient, if not the only, way to eradicate poverty. This transformation reinforced the idea that material prosperity is the primary goal to which other concerns should be secondary. This change started inside the prevalent Anglo component of the American culture, but it invaded also to a certain degree the cultural heritage of minorities living in the U.S.A., even though these are inclined to preserve their own culture. Marketing has been systematically extended towards Blacks, Hispanics and lately Asians, in the same way it has been directed towards children. All are potential consumers and marketing consultants develop the best strategies to get their money. Advertising now presents black, brown or yellow faces along with white. Through consumption the principles of the market impose their primacy on different cultural backgrounds. **Daily at the local, national, and global level, we see the switch from cultural principles born from religious and humanistic values to cultural principles coming from market functioning.**

Out of the womb of the market, a new reality took life which suffocated the values rooted in the Greco-Latin and Judeo-Christian human-centered visions of life, that took centuries to benefit more than a few free men, citizens, or land owners. In these cultures the trend was to make the human person the reference for most decisions. Similarly, the values and wisdom of Asians entering this country more recently have also been eroded by the market culture. This shifting toward obedience to market mechanisms was made easier by the first immigrants' caution about social relationships. Wounded in Europe by dysfunctional secular or ecclesiastical relationships, the first settlers carried with them an anthropology where relationships were not essential for becoming a human being fully whole. I feel this still prevails in the U.S. culture.[26] The individualism exemplified in the role model of the self-made man helped society move from a human centered vision of life to market mechanisms, where human relationships have less and less importance.[27] At the opposite pole the traditional Christian anthropology proclaimed relationships are the medium for a human being to develop one's humanness. This one is not innate; it is through relationships that an individual becomes a person. This will be discussed more fully in a later chapter.

Characteristics of the Market Culture

For understanding better the emergent *market culture* a comparison with the *human based cultures* is beneficial. Neither of these two types of culture is a monolith. The market culture continues to evolve rapidly. On the other hand, there is more than one human based culture. Differences between the human based cultures from the Greco-Latin world, those from Asia, or those alive in the Native American Nations are obvious. Nevertheless, they have common characteristics. However, the contrast and sometimes the opposition between human based cultures, as they were in the first half of the twentieth century, and market culture as at the end of the twentieth century, may help us to comprehend what really has changed. It may become clearer by observing how each of these cultures perceives work, persons, society, relationships, and cultural goals.

A human based culture considers **work** a means to provide one's necessities, to express one's gifts, and to contribute to one's society. Society needs the diverse gifts of all its members in order to function healthfully and easily. Pursuing such aims through work the person becomes more integrated, even when the work is back-breaking. A market culture, on the other hand, sees **work** mainly as a means of making money through one's activity, and to produce things not necessarily fulfilling a real human need. This mentality allows corporate executives to close or relocate factories to where low wages are the norm, without considering the needs of their present employees.

A human based culture sees the individual **becoming a person** through the dynamic of relationships. No person is an island. A person lives within a network or web of exchanges: with other humans, with God, with other creatures, and even with one's dark side. The need for these relationships is expressed in philosophical reflection, institutions, and the models the human based culture offers to the oncoming generations. The market culture has objectified its constituency and recognizes the **individuals primarily as producers**

and consumers. In the case of the factory closures, as in the case of corn production in Guatemala, we encounter this reduction of the human person to the utilitarian aspect of its existence.

Human based cultures see **society** as the indispensable medium for the development of the human being. They challenge societies to work at becoming a more perfect place of communion and become the ripened fruit of humankind. In the market culture, however, **society** is seen as a pragmatic medium, temporarily useful. Individuals know what their needs are. Society should avoid promoting an ideology or referring to a common good. In reality, market society gives birth to a subtle ideology and influences the wants and needs of people.

About **relationships,** most human based cultures see any being, animate or inanimate, with a certain respect and reverence. A kind of awe, sometimes a holy fear, gives to people the understanding that they are relating to a sacred presence, which many call God. The European religious and humanistic background of the first settlers had lost part of their reverence of the primitive cultures, but still had strong respect for human beings, at least if they were whites. In the market culture **relationships** are mainly utilitarian. The earth and its resources are at the disposal of whoever wants them. Most of the time persons are considered mere commodities.[28] Any sense of sacredness is foreign to the good functioning of these utilitarian relationships. In the example taken from the functioning of hospitals, the patient is considered an object.

The human based cultures see the **goal of the culture** as favoring a holistic development of the human beings and of the societies created by the persons. The **market culture's goal** favors material development and economic prosperity.

Ethicist voices are considered incompetent to address the subject. The rationalism of the market laws should be followed if material bankruptcy is to be avoided.

These contrasts are schematic and a little overcontrasted. Yet, I feel they are fairly accurate. The human based cultures might look too idealized, as their recent failures are too obvious: the subproletariat, the colonial wars, the Shoah, etc. These failures, however, do not contradict the attempt of the majority of people to be faithful to the principles giving the *raison d'etre* to the culture. In the market culture, the material functioning of the market society becomes a substitute for moral principles.

Nevertheless, no person belongs fully to one of the two cultures illustrated above. People who adopt the new values coming from the market system continue to enflesh some of the values of the human based culture. That double allegiance is responsible for much of the double language, which covers new realities with words from the previous cultures. It increases the ambiguity of various situations. We will see how the changes from one to the other happened.

Substitution of Principles: From Human-based Culture to Market System

Having noted the consequences of the market culture, a series of examples may help in understanding how the substitution of principles happened at the international, national, and local level.

On the international level, the "structural adjustment" policy of the World Bank illustrates the substitution of market laws for moral principles. In recent decades, the World Bank required from countries asking for important loans that they comply with strict demands concerning their economy. The goal is to secure payment of interests and reimbursement of the capital. In reality it gives enormous powers to the World Bank. Protests from borrowing countries and from a coalition of first world countries organizations formed at the occasion of the 50th anniversary of the Bretton Woods agreememts[29] produce only slow results. Any revision of the World Bank's principles is out of the question according to western econo-mists. In reality the World Bank was established on free market and material development principles. The humanistic and religious roots have disappeared.[30] In developing coun-tries throughout the centuries the economy of subsistence allowed families a minimum of food. World Bank requests the country to favor cash crops and industries in order to export and have foreign currencies. Practically this replaces the economy of subsistence which does not enter into the market flow of exchanges. Hundreds of millions of people are suffer-ing the consequences of the "structural adjustment" imposed by the World Bank upon their government. Like a straight jacket this adjustment makes their survival more difficult, restricts the previous way of life, and strangles the values formerly revered. The new values are presented as essential for the well being of the country in an international context dominated by economic competition. In reality the goal of the financial advisors is threefold, to pay back the loans contracted by governments which bought military hardware, to satisfy the eagerness of a small minority in copying the American Way of Life, and to incorporate the country into the "free market" and its global trade. The model of develop-ment promoted by the "structural adjustment" is not the *integral development* directed towards the wholeness of the human persons. Some countries have tried to establish other models recommended inside or outside the United Nations, but these have not been accepted. The World Bank centers its vision and goals in order to increase the gross national product and exports, even though the price on humans is very high.

Worried by these violent policies against the less developed countries some Christian communities of seven Third World nations in 1989 published the Kairos document decrying these developments. They were dismayed that Christians of the First World did not answer appropriately to their cry which arose from the gravity of the situation of their people.

The dramatic consequences of these events abroad shed light on what is happening at home. On the national level market laws also impose their dictates over all other principles. During the discussions in the U.S. Congress regarding welfare reform in 1996, concern for society's weakest individuals—the pride of North Americans after Franklin Delano Roosevelt—was ignored. FDR pushed legislation that expressed a deep humanist concern which could be found in the soul of most citizens. It has been replaced by a narrow accounting which cuts welfare for many vulnerable people, especially the handicapped and children. Social services are the first victims of a balanced budget, rather than trimming subsidies to agribusiness and ending tax favors for large corporations.[31] This "corporate welfare" remains unchallenged in the budgetary process. The official rationale is that these large corporations bring needed jobs. It might happen for a few years. Later, however, corporate beneficiaries of the "corporate welfare" may move to other countries for greater profit without any protest from the government.

On the local level, the laws of market presented as almost divine prevent many low-income people from affording lodging, in contrast to the previous policy that made access to home ownership easy. The right to lodging is a basic human right. Most religions proclaim that this right should be respected. Nevertheless, an impressive number of vacant buildings are inaccessible because the rights of private property and market laws pretend to have priority over any moral or religious principles. For example, in Las Vegas, where in 1996 officials recognized at least 15,000 homeless, five hotels with a total of 6,000 rooms have in less than three years been demolished to make space for new, more profitable hotel-casinos. Why was it out of the question to consider an administrative or social use of these not-so-old buildings? Similarly, in the Presidio of San Francisco 466 well-maintained apartments vacated by military families would have been razed had not a coalition of churches organized a long campaign of protests.[32]

Often I hear parents complain that they do not understand where their children found the values for their life. These are totally foreign to what was taught at home. For example, money is the main factor for changing jobs while the consequences on the family are not a first priority. Parents are stunned when they learn that their children do not want to have a family. A concept of honesty at the work place or towards the IRS frequently held by the older generation often conflicts with the behavior of their offspring.

The reality is that children and their parents or grandparents belong to two different worlds, each of which has its own culture. Financial interests control the media, popular music and entertainment, and cast their values upon the children, who receive through these channels their main teachings on moral norms.[33] A true metastasis develops inside the American Way of Life as it was lived in the middle of this century. The result is a growing subservient mass of people whose culture is now the Market Culture.

A frightening change of principles occurred in the successive uses of the word **freedom.** For the country's forefathers, freedom meant exemption from the control of arbitrary power, religious or political. This included the ability to act without restraint. Clearly, for the secessionist colonies this first meaning included the absence of an authoritative control over trade and religious choices. In a very different manner, when President George Bush announced the beginning of the Gulf War in 1991, he equated the defense of freedom with "the defense of our way of life," which required defense of free market and the circulation of goods. Evidence indicates that most politicians today consider free market the backbone of freedom. Is it not a completely different meaning from that which existed at the beginning of this country?

I have often witnessed what happens to immigrants when they arrive in this country. At the beginning most of their daily choices are still influenced by the culture they brought with them. If they dwell in an ethnic neighborhood, as many Latin Americans or Asians do, or if they belong to an ethnic network, their way of life follows many patterns of their country of origin. As soon as their children—through the influence of their peers, the movie industry and television programming—are submitted to the subtle brainwashing of advertisement, the principles of the market culture penetrate the life of the whole family. Immigrant refugees, originally fascinated by the ideal of freedom, are more and more seduced by the glitter of abundance. The immigrants' cultural influence decreases in the name of a so-called "melting pot" where in fact the dominant Anglo-Saxon group dissolves the recently brought values as if they were destructive to national cohesion. Present legislations against bilingualism are one of many examples. The whole immigrant family adopts what the hosting culture presents in practical daily living as the heart of freedom: the freedom to buy what they want; the freedom to have more wants and to satisfy them; the so-called freedom to have market values leading the whole of their life, even if it means the sacrifice of precious relationships.

As illustrated above, a market culture is **a culture where the laws of the market economy, presently dominated by the free market theory, take the place of the principles on which previous cultures had been established.** Our cultural edifice may still look like the one of the past, and people may believe the foundations of their culture are the same, but in reality a radical change has happened. Without it being noticed the old values receded and were replaced by completely different priorities coming from the womb of the market. The trading post, a useful accessory to a culture, has disappeared. The well-organized market with its rationalism has taken its place, not as an accessory but as the very backbone of our present U.S. culture.

No one could challenge the statement that the first country to develop a market culture is the U.S. Within the U.S. and various other countries, more and more people now notice the dramatic consequences of U.S. leadership in promoting and spreading such a culture. The rhetoric of the Ayatollah Khomeini and others against the American Way of Life is only an extremist manifestation of rampant and less publicized reactions. During the discussions on international agreements or conventions, many ordinary North Americans are shocked by the change of values shown by their government. In front of an international quasi consensus, U.S. representatives are often alone in defending policies judged immoral by a majority of their constituency. Those who elected them realize the substitution of values inside the cultural treasure of their country.[34] The government neglects national and international public opinion as shown by its position on the land mines ban, the environmental decisions of Rio de Janeiro, or decisions by the World Court in Den Haag [35] to cite only a few examples. The government is aware that it can disregard public opinion because most protesters continue to abide by and nurture the market culture in their daily buying choices. This dissenters' inconsistency can be seen in the waste of energy, in transportation, house building, or in the number of electrical appliances used. This style of life supports the new values, and helps the growing grip of the market laws over our lives.

The Violence Flowing from the Market Culture

Sadly, I witness that through the aggressive trade policy of the U.S. the market culture spreads all over the globe, bringing prosperity to a few, while imposing a disrespect of the wisdom and uniqueness of host cultures. I saw this deprivation in every one of the nine Latin American countries I visited, as well as in Europe when I returned for a short while. I encountered French, Italians, Spaniards, Germans and Austrians who told me what they lost in buying various American products and accepting their methods of marketing. I also heard Asians, Africans, and Australians making similar reflections. Normally in one's own culture each person finds an ease and a feeling of being in a well-known territory. Culture gives the security of a maternal womb for the social growth of persons. This allows individuals to let their identity develop in a familiar context and as part of a specific group. In contrast, when the wisdom and uniqueness of a culture are despised and replaced by a global market culture, people lose their points of reference and feel disoriented, uprooted, and even violated. Guatemalan and Salvadoran refugees in this country or in Canada provided me painful examples of the need for one's own culture. I encountered many whose culture shock worsened with their perception that the way of life they were now taking advantage of was an important cause of the violence in their homeland. Many preferred to return. A Guatemalan friend who gained political asylum in Toronto told me clearly that he could not survive in a culture so destructive of the main values of his own culture. He preferred to risk himself and his family in his own country, even to face anew the death squads. He escaped them only because of international accompaniment.

The rising and mushrooming of the market culture represents a violence of dramatic intensity and magnitude towards people of other cultures, both inside the U.S. and wherever this industrial giant penetrates other parts of the world. Those who are fathering these developments may be smiling persons speaking softly, but their violence devastates those who suffer from it. The violence flowing from the market culture affects the core of any creature: human or other created being. Following its utilitarian principles, the market culture does not value the preciousness or sacredness of all creatures. This disrespect births in its victims a profound frustration often difficult to identify, but one that awakens violent responses.

We lament that this violence imposed by the market culture is so rarely mentioned. The violence resulting from market mechanisms is more than economic unbalance or poverty imposed on some people. It is more than violence imposed on persons vulnerable to advertising who unwillingly become consumers. It deprives people of the nurturing environment that their culture gave to them. Anyone experiencing a cultural change can be distressed by the culture shock. When de-culturized people are submitted to an environment which has no place for the mysterious, the indescribable within a human, the situation becomes dramatic. When a materialistic culture replaces a culture based on humanness, destruction follows. The countries that have been submitted to the Marxist ideological materialism give us matters for reflection. The destruction done by the materialism of the market culture goes deep inside the person.

When a culture becomes driven primarily by monetary gain, it sees human and creation's resources as objects to be used for amassing wealth. The result is a loss of the sense of the sacred. Life is devalued. There is a desensitizing of awareness of the destruction and death that violence inflicts on both the victim and the perpetrator.

In his landmark work, *I and Thou*, Martin Buber recognizes the tendencies toward objectifying life and the loss of relational reality. With reference to economic life he says:

> Man's will to profit and will to power are natural and legitimate as long as they are tied to the will to human relations and carried by it. . . . The economy as the house of the will to profit and the State as the house of the will to power participate in life as long as they participate in the spirit. If they abjure the spirit, they abjure life.[36]

Is our market culture losing its "participation in the spirit"? In Buber's terms, is it losing its sense of the significance of the relational dimensions of human life, losing its sense of the sacred? The events mentioned at the beginning of this chapter seem to indicate such a trend.

What Is at Stake: The Sacred, the Human

What is at stake when I speak of "sacred"? I have been amazed by what comes to people's mind when I use the words "sacred" or "sacredness." For many it suggests special places, where contact with the divine can be experienced, such as mountains, springs, churches and temples, or special locations such as the Holy of Holies, the Holy Sacrament, or the Holy Stone of Mecca. However, many religious traditions, especially the Judeo-Christian, do not limit the sacred to special places. Instead they proclaim all of life is sacred because it belongs to God. Within these traditions some human relationships have also been proclaimed particularly sacred, which means very profoundly revered, in the understanding that God has witnessed their celebration such as vows, marriage, oaths or treaties.

Even when the sacred was not respected, it was most often recognized that it should be respected. With this limit, in the past, a sacred respect was given to love between partners, to defenseless children, to parent's love for their offspring, and to children's respect for their parents. The recognition of sacredness was expressed by reverence and, if needed, immunity, as it was shown in taking refuge in a sanctuary against the pursuit of a killer. The presence of God was recognized and God's law was perceived as sacred. Relationship with such a mysterious and awesome Presence is the foundation of the sacred. Consciousness of a reality far beyond our common experience and knowledge opens the door to the precious pearl of our existence. It is our experience of transcendence. It is what gives value to life in the present and hope for the world's future.

The word humanness refers to what makes a human being a truly human person. It is the preciousness, the dignity, which is directly related to sacredness. There is a wide consensus on the globe that the human being has an intrinsic dignity. The Universal Declaration of Human Rights of the U.N. formalized this consensus.[37] Biologists relate this dignity to the special place of the human body in the biological evolution, and its sophisticated neurological system. For Christians it is shown by the Incarnation, the presence in a human body of a person of the divine family, Jesus Christ.

The market culture frequently collides with sacredness and humanness. Its birth and development became possible when quantification took a central place within the Western culture. Recent centuries have seen the growing influence of the world of quantification. Mathematical abstractions and formulas allowed the development of "exact" science and of technology. While the power of humankind grew considerably with the use of the quantifying approach, thinkers of many fields point out the limits and the destructiveness of a general and often exclusive use of the quantifying model. The market society using quantifying tools developed in a prodigious manner, while focus on quality and reverence for life eroded. A culture based on market principles now imposes its values on us and dictates our behaviors. It claims an exclusive expertise in economic matters and then proclaims the inevitability of its values and methods.

Greed, Casualness, Prejudices, Ignoring Sacredness

Coming from a very secularized country, I was amazed and I am still shocked in reading on coins and dollar bills the imprint "In God We Trust." The economy operates with no serious questions about what these words might mean in setting priorities for its functioning. In the market culture in which we live, reference to God or to the divine is superficial. The major focus is material prosperity. Development and profit are the supreme values that justify choices. John Kavanaugh has brilliantly shown how advertising uses altruism, love, feelings for children, and attraction to the woman's body for making money at the expense of the mystery that is at the core of each person.[38] Human beings become mere commodities. It is not rhetoric to call this a true prostitution!

Such prostitution is pervasive in our market culture. Workers who did not have other alternative than to work at the Nevada Test Site making nuclear tests possible, or as a dealer or manager in a Las Vegas casino, told me their feelings and the moral questions that came from their job that shows a wrong priority of values. Do we not all feel violated—prostituted—in adhering to certain policies established upon principles we reject ? When domestic policies crush the poor and defenseless, or international policies take advantage of poor countries through international agreements like G.A.T.T. or N.A.F.T.A., who calls in the vice squads to stop the prostitution and arrest those who benefit from it? Can people in a market culture hear the thunder of Amos—"let justice roll like waters"? Television viewers can lament the plight of the poor and shortly after vote for proponents of these violent market structures that make the life of the poor more miserable. Are they unable to see or unwilling to face the relationship between the policies and their consequences? Have they been brainwashed to believe that the laws of the market culture are in fact the laws of the universe, divine laws that should not be resisted? And the prostitution goes on.

The devaluation of life in a market culture is further demonstrated in the casualness of killings between gang members for the exclusive right to sell drugs in an area, or of deadly attacks for a few dollars. Are gang members just following the behavior of political and financial leaders or sports and entertainment heroes who set the tone of the cultural values? When money is idolized, whether in corporate boardrooms, legislative halls, television or movies, or in the street gangs, human life is cheapened. Greed makes people unconcerned and indifferent to human life. A market culture, captive to an exclusive concern for profit making without any thought for the millions of people victimized by choices being made, begins to see this situation as normal. Speculators, untroubled by their conscience as they follow the "supreme" laws of the market, can prey on groups or nations. Moral questions are further avoided as their computer software directs the buy and sell orders without personal involvement of their conscience and will in the decision.

There are other examples of the casualness and loss of respect for life that should be noted. Deaths on the roads, abortions by affluent healthy parents whose choice comes from no other reason than to protect their comfort, death penalty imposed for an illusory security, capital executions offered as just another television show, presentations of first strike weapons as technical prowess, or reprisals justified as normal answers to an aggression—all are symptoms of the same prevalent casualness that has grown up on the materialist ground of the market culture.

Besides greed and casualness, racial and national prejudices also reflect a loss of the sense of the sacredness of all life. Many countries with people of color know well that in the eyes of the market culture the lives of their citizens are not as valuable as the lives of those who built and continue to spread such a culture. For example, in reporting the casualties in a war, an accident or a natural disaster, the North American media values the life of **one** US. citizen more than many lives from a Third World country. The ratio of interest might be 1 to 100, 1 to 1,000 or more; it does not matter. This reveals a lack of awareness that sacredness of life knows neither racial nor national boundaries. In other cases an event is reported only when there is a large number of victims. Our materialist assumption about quantity has eroded the reality of the reverence due to life. No longer is it accepted that within every human being there is a mystery where the divine dwells.

A few years ago our Pace e Bene Center worked with more than fifteen groups pursuing social transformation. Our aim was to help these groups in identifying the obstacles to their action coming from the culture and to examine how they were overcoming these realities. Almost all the groups mentioned de-humanization as an important obstacle, and six groups placed it as the most destructive of all. A series of meetings was held with these groups and a deeper search was conducted. The various processes of dehumanization destroy the relatedness needed for being fully human. People "are treated as non-human by the larger society. "You do not count." "You have lost in the great game of life." "You are expendable." "You are not human." These are the messages that homeless persons, gang members, minorities, poor of various kinds, Appalachians, and Native Americans receive day in and day out when applying for a job, when requesting aid or when encountering other people. . . . "We are dehu-manized when we are the victims or the perpetrators of the key cultural assumption of superiority."[39]

My mind is full of examples of such casualness in dealing with persons and realities that were respected before the former cultures were submerged by the market mentality and its greed, prejudices and quantification. Let us not be hasty to accuse technical progress which by itself does not require the loss of humanness. Greed and technology do not necessarily have to go hand in hand, but technology can give greed an incredible power to pursue its aim of making money by any means in the shortest amount of time.

In comparing the market culture with the previous cultures, I am not blind to so many violations of sacredness that previous cultures had shown: slavery for centuries before being eliminated from the Christian world proclaiming the Gospel; serfdom, massacres and wars; obscene richness of kings or princes are only a few of the flaws inside the Judeo-Christian world in centuries past. It is worth noting that when people were not practicing what they preached about the human being, most of the time they nevertheless did not modify the proclaimed principles. They might have closed their eyes or their heart. In contrast the market culture changed the points of reference, the principles for a human life. It changed not only the practice, but the preaching.

Violence and Erosion of the Sacred

We lament that little attention has been given to understanding the relationships between the erosion of sacredness, the casualness toward life, and the various manifestations of violence in our market culture. The above examples invite us to look at these connections more carefully. Like a cancer, casualness invades the sacred space within ourselves and makes us unable to recognize in other human beings the sacredness that is their humanness, their dignity.

Sacredness likewise dwells within all created beings, for they are our brothers and sisters: brother sun, sister moon, brothers and sisters the stars, the animals, the plants, the minerals, sister water, brother wind, as St. Francis named them tenderly in his Canticle of the Creatures.

Only the persons who recognize and accept the mystery of this sacred presence inside themselves can show reverence for the sacred in other humans and in the whole of creation. Such persons, humbly greeting the divine within and around them, express in their words and actions the power of the spirit that can counter the desecration of creation. In Christian terms when we are in touch with the Spirit of God inside us, then the Spirit enables us to recognize God's presence in others. Conversely, the non-recognition of sacredness within the self blinds us to the sacredness in others and contributes to the escalation of violence.

Remedies to Destructive Desecration?

Dumbfounded by the overwhelming lack of reverence for the sacred in our culture, we seek remedies to deter us from such a destructive path. Against the erosion of sacredness, some people have placed their hope in moral imperatives based on religion or traditions. This method clearly has not been able to slow down the destructive process. This failure of moralism with its "you must" and "you have to" is predictable *because neither ethics nor a sterile moralism gives a foundation to sacredness;* rather sacredness provides a basis for ethics and especially the foundation for any morality of integrity. In any case, to search for a direct remedy might be a waste of time. We live in a pragmatic cultural context, consequently it might be only through the pursuit of practical results that most of the inner realities can be rediscovered and accepted.

Change in our world requires an inner rebellion against what oppresses our own sacredness and the sacredness or dignity of other people. When Miguel d'Escoto,[40] fasting in Managua in 1985, called the Christians to a "Gospel insurrection," I think it was that rebellion he was speaking about. **No human being is for sale.** Let us not accept having our inner treasure offered for sale. That inner treasure is God's presence in the depth of ourselves and at the center of every human being even when that human acts despicably. Even inside the worst of criminals God dwells and that presence makes the death penalty so immoral and anti human. The movie *Dead Man Walking* reminded us of that deep truth. I experienced the truth of that presence both in encountering former inmates of the infamous French "bagne" of Guyana, and in meeting Guatemalan collaborators of torture.

The market culture which claims to be the culture of the future does not recognize the sacredness that is the most valuable treasure of every created being: humans, of course, but also their brothers and sisters such as plants, animals, mountains and rivers, which owe their existence to the same God.

I mentioned how many people suffer from a dehumanizing process. In fact the dehumanization that accompanies the global phenomenon of urbanization is largely the product of the market culture. When people sense that their preciousness and their dignity are not recognized, they feel deprived of their humanness, they feel de-humanized and sometimes express their frustration against the violence of the market culture with violent acts.

As a remedy to desecration of the human being, the daily actions that can help people retrieve their humanness are of major importance. Being considered a precious person whose dignity is indestructible invites people to a more humane behavior, more respectful of justice, and more peaceful. Hundreds of millions of market culture victims wait for suggestions and help in retrieving their humanness. Will they encounter enough support in their critical quest?

Questions for Reflection

- *What do you feel is most important in this chapter?*

- *What is stirred in you by this chapter?*

- *Do you find difficulty in recognizing and accepting the mystery of the sacred presence inside yourself? Why? Recall events that made you recognize that your own dignity is related to the mystery in you—something of God.*

- *What ways could avoid the strengthening of the market culture?*

- *How could nonviolence accept the existence of the market society and still refuse to admit that the market set of values invades the field of cultural values?*

- *Are you supporting civic structures and corporations that respect humanistic principles? Alternative food, alternative manufacturing, alternative markets, alternative services?*

- *Do you struggle against corporations, media and political structures that are founded on the principles of the market culture?*

CHAPTER FOUR

Seeds of Violence from Colonial Origin

HAVING NOTED THE EMERGENCE of the market culture and its consequent desecration of humanness, we now turn our attention to seeking understanding of how the new market culture is related to the colonial origins of the U.S., and in what ways those realities became seeds of the violence in the culture.

In France I read epic events about the coming to America of the Dutch, the British, the Spaniards and the French. I knew a little about the thirteen Colonies and the struggle for independence. I knew more about the Louisiana Purchase. But I did not have any idea about the scars left by this colonial period.

In Chicago, shortly after my arrival, I experienced some scars of the U.S. colonial origin. Our community was in a multiethnic neighborhood including 12,000 Native Americans who had been "transferred" into that area after World War II. Returning from the army with no prospective jobs on the Indian reservations, they had been invited to board special trains to cities where they would find "plenty of jobs." Twenty-five years later, many of them were my day laborer companions. I heard the pain of people deprived of their style of life and deceived by the American Administration. In the same neighborhood a few thousand Blacks and a larger number of Hispanics from various countries coexisted with former coal miners from Appalachia, all hoping for work in the industry capital. They were all part of the underclass that started with the colonial era.

More recently I have been supporting the struggles of several native tribes or First Nations: the Shoshone Dann band in northern Nevada, the Western Shoshone National Council at the Nuclear Test Site, and the Timbisha Shoshone tribe of Death Valley. I was also close to traditionalist Navajos resisting their uprooting at Big Mountain in Arizona. Through these friendships and activities of support I learned more about how the U.S. administration treated Native Americans. Administrative rigidity, arrogance, breaking of promises, collusion with big corporations, and even lies from those in charge of implementing the Constitution and treaties, brought me the most discouraging moments of my life.

Five centuries after the "discovery" of the New World and the development of European colonies a more accurate evaluation can be made of colonialism's beneficial and harmful consequences. Successively, the main European countries entered into that ambiguous adventure, a nation overtaking other territories and their inhabitants. Some colonial founders had religious motivations, mainly a certain misreading of the Christian mission to evangelize and baptize all nations. Explorers and missionaries came overseas to open the doors of heaven to "savages" who otherwise, they said, would have an uncertain or terrible future. Others advanced philosophical or humanitarian motives, struggling against famine, mortality and tribal wars, in the colonized territories. Others claimed they were bringing the benefits of civilization with its useful knowledge and techniques. Some others said, either cautiously or openly, they wanted to become richer or make their country more powerful. Whatever the motives, even when it was "for the good of the colony's Natives" and whatever benefits were received, the former occupants of colonized lands became victims of violence from the new-comers.

In every colonizing country—Spain, Portugal, England, Netherlands, France, Germany, Italy—opponents perceived the destructive aspects in colonizing a territory, importing a language and imposing on the inhabitants a new way of life and even a religion. Some were conscious that the economic development of these lands was organized to benefit the mother country, not mainly for the good of the natives. Social structures, agricultural wisdom, and economic practices of the indigenous people were forced to change. In France human rights defenders expressed indignation against colo-nialism, and this was true regarding the American colonies also. Unfortunately, too often Christians blinded by the mis-sion to evangelize did not join the opposition to the colonial adventure. During the 18th and the 19th centuries the colo-nial empires built in the New World by France, England, Spain and Portugal gradually crumbled. After World War II a tidal wave of decolonization swept over the remaining em-pires of England, France, and the Netherlands. Deep reflec-tions on what had been destroyed by colonizers emerged. The quincentennial commemoration of the "discovery" of the Americas by Christopher Columbus brought to light little known documents of the past that weighed to the negative side of the scale of justice. Inside the colonial nations more people started to beat their chest.

My purpose is not to elaborate further upon the responsi-bilities of the colonizers and the direct or indirect sufferings of the colonized, but to examine, from my experience, the violent consequences of the colonial origin on U.S. culture today.

Racist Legacy of the Colonial Era

In Nevada I have various friendships with Western Shoshones. The large Shoshone ethnic group is present also in Montana, part of Utah, and Idaho. The Western Shoshones, living on a smaller area, have a history of their own. When the first Whites penetrated their territory around 1820, the Shoshones were mainly bands of hunters and gatherers moving from one place to the other, following the seasons. Their huge territory included the eastern half of Nevada, a large part of southern California, and a small part of southern Idaho. The first conflicts with Whites arose when fur hunters killed the animals the Shoshone's needed for food. When the travelers joining the Gold Rush fever in California passed through the Shoshone territory, their carelessness and their violence added more incidents.

After signing a peace and friendship treaty in 1855, U.S. representatives and various Shoshone Band chiefs signed the treaty of Ruby Valley in 1863. In this treaty, registered as an international treaty in the U.S. Congress, the Shoshone authorized the traveling and settling of Whites on their territory, but did not give, cede, sell or trade land with the U.S. The Shoshones soon realized that U.S. officials considered all Shoshone land as federal property and disposed of it in whatever manner they liked. The Native people's sacred land was used for military purposes or sold to developers. Finally, in 1946 Congress established the Indian Claims Commission to hear and resolve Natives' claims arising from the U.S. take over of their land. In 1966 U.S. authorities arbitrarily declared that the extinction of the Western Shoshone title to over 22 millions acres of land in Nevada took place in 1872. They established an amount of money, priced in 1872 value(!!), for the land. The Western Shoshones refused the deal and proclaimed land cannot be sold. The U.S. laws, however, prevailed; one law maintains that the Shoshone's legal representative is the Secretary of Interior of the Government with whom they signed the treaty! Notwithstanding this scandalous conflict of interests, the Secretary of Interior accepted *in the name of the Shoshones* the money that, as member of the Government, he decided to ascribe to them! The money refused by the Shoshones is still waiting in an escrow account. The Shoshones are angry because they were considered children, unable to make a decision. The Secretary of Interior decided what monies the Natives should receive. As their trustee, he accepted it. In 1992, in a letter to Mr. Lujan, Jr., then the Secretary of Interior, an elder of the Western Shoshone Nation, Carrie Dann wrote, "Today in 1992, 500 years after Columbus' first visit to the Americas, the Western Shoshones still don't have rights to land and they are still looked upon as animals by the U.S. Supreme court, and many in the legislative, judicial and executive branches of the U.S. government as well. . . . In my opinion, the thinking of the U.S. Supreme Court puts us into the category of non-human." Other elders of the Shoshone nation expressed similar statements which were corroborated by their lawyers, and even by representatives of the U.S. administration.

In their relationships with the U.S. administration, the Shoshones refer frequently to the Treaty of 1863, and ask the administration to show their proof of ownership, which does not exist.

Unfortunately, the Shoshone case is not isolated. Many other documented expressions of racism towards Native

Americans exist. Some are in the laws and regulations, as in the example cited above, when they are required to have a trustee who does not need their acceptance. In the eyes of the law they are considered children. Other racist expressions are encountered daily. Many North Americans have a patronizing tenderness towards the Natives. They have compassion for them as victims of repeated injustices; and at the same time, they often manifest a feeling of superiority, as if Natives are at best second-rate humans. This is a mark of racism.

This specific racism toward the Indians grew directly from this country's colonial past. From the first landing of Europeans on the North American soil, the colonizers' mentality birthed economic structures and laws that expressed their thinking. Christopher Columbus made it clear. In his journal describing the Arawak people he wrote: "They would make fine servants. . . . With fifty men we could subjugate them all and make them do whatever we want." Columbus promised the King and the Queen "as much gold as they need . . . and as many slaves as they ask." In 1495 Columbus took 1500 Native people in Hispaniola to serve as slaves and shipped 500 to Spain.

Sadly, the U.S. administration violated many international treaties signed between Americans and Indian Nations or Tribes. It substantiates the words of Columbus. Now it weighs on the conscience of many North Americans who feel guilty for so many injustices. More than that, it introduced in the North American praxis a relativization of the most solemn oaths when U.S. interest is at stake.[41] It also reinforces a practical contempt of non-Whites.

Not every manifestation of racism stems from colonial origins. Racism against Hispanics, Asians, or Arabs reflects the fear and insecurity a majority group feels as it observes the growing development, strength and unique differences of a minority group. When the majority fears losing a privileged status, intolerance increases.

Most colonizers, living within their country of origin, would have found slave ownership and even more slave importation unacceptable, despite Christopher Columbus' example. But the necessities of agricultural development silenced their Christian moral principles. In these new territories it became acceptable to kidnap black people in Africa and ship them like animals in order to make them slaves to cultivate a vast rich land. Through a long courageous struggle, slavery ended and civil rights triumphed; yet prejudices against the African Americans still exist within many Whites; the country's economic structures continue to favor Whites.

It is no wonder that Native Americans and African Americans are often deeply frustrated. Their anger arises from their wounded pride and dignity, and doubt about their worth, as their humanity has been denied so often. Native Americans and Hispanics told me frequently how the generation of their parents and sometimes grandparents, ashamed of their origin, tried hard to behave and look like Euro-Americans. For Blacks, the lighter your complexion was the better. Native Americans avoided teaching their native language and traditions to their children, who now are proud to learn it. Wounds and anger are among the most frequent causes of violence. Victims of ever-present structural violence turn their anger and despair against their own lives. Feeling worthless, they try to forget their shame by turning to alcohol. On the reservations, Native youths commit suicide at a high rate. Superficial observers declare these people responsible when they explode violently, forgetting that the subtle and covert violence of a mentality and of its economic, legal, and civic structures is a prior violence and the one responsible for open violence. While Equal Opportunity Employment improved some situations, it nevertheless has not resolved all cases of job and lodging discrimination.

Another manifestation of racism that arose from the origins of the country is the high percentage of minorities, especially Black people, in the U.S. prisons. Victims of unemployment, Blacks are often arrested more quickly than Caucasians.[42] When a crime is committed, a frequent reflex is to search for a Black perpetrator. Juries send more African Americans than members of any other ethnic group to prison and death row.

Our Franciscan community is located in the black neighborhood of Las Vegas. Around our house we can see plenty of unemployed Blacks. In 1992 when a court acquitted the white policeman who beat up Rodney King in Los Angeles, many understood the court decision as a message, "It is not a crime to beat up a Black." Riots erupted first in Los Angeles. The following afternoon in Las Vegas, African Americans gathered and walked towards City Hall to protest this scandalous judgment. The police impeded them from leaving the "black ghetto," fearing that they might ransack and burn the downtown casinos. Some arsonists and looters joined the blocked demonstrators. Various administrative and commercial buildings in the black community were set afire. The police blockaded the neighborhood making it impossible to enter or leave. They decreed a curfew limited to this neighborhood. The following day local authorities declared a new curfew for our area. After a huge concert of protest against this discriminatory measure, singling out the black neighborhood, City Hall reversed its shocking decision and invented something that you can only see in Las Vegas: "a **voluntary curfew** for all the city," which of course was not implemented.

Black ghettos and Indian reservations are a powder keg. The racism inherited from the colonial era continues to accumulate more explosive power! African American leaders express the view that, after the significant step of the Civil Rights legislation, no noticeable progress in respect, esteem and power happened. No big economic and behavioral changes have occurred in the society at large. Similarly, Native Americans do not see a significant change in the laws and behaviors of Whites. Black unemployment is very high, and they resent it. Natives, stimulated by the celebration of the Quincentennial of Columbus' landing in Hispaniola, are more and more conscious of the violence done to their people.[43]

From time to time some revealing events showing the depth of the racism against Blacks seem to awaken a few Whites, but for how long? The celebration of the quincentennial of "Columbus' discovery" of America unexpectedly brought painful events of the past to the conscience of Whites, and started a process that could bring change in White consciousness and mentality. In this growing consciousness resides the hope for healing the profound wound inside the culture and its structures.[44]

An Oppressed People Who Became Oppressive

Violence rooted in the colonial past transcends the domestic scene. When I led workshops or gave conferences in Latin America, I often heard the question, "Why does the U.S.A. make us suffer so much?" People referred to the economic colonialism imposed on their countries, or to the aid given to their oppressive governments. Suffering people challenged me to make North Americans more aware of their government's actions. I heard this cry when accompanying people who were targets of the death squads in Guatemala; or in Oruro, Bolivia, talking late at night with a priest, who spoke passionately about the fate of miners who were victims of falling tin prices. Such decisions were made in Chicago or New York City. I heard the same cry in Mexico during a workshop shortly after the Zapatista insurrection in Chiapas. It is hard to receive the precious cry of these wounded people pointing out the source of the violence they suffer and telling me that I benefit from it. Though unpleasant to hear, it is true!

How can such an imperialist spirit sustain the foreign policy of the U.S.A., a country once a victim of British colonialism? Modern psychology partially answers the question by noting that victims of abuse and oppression tend to victimize others. Is this pattern also part of the life of societies? Do formerly oppressed societies become oppressive when they do not face their wounds openly? Do they impose on others the same suffering that was theirs? Examples of other nations indicate a positive answer to these questions. Not only do some abused children become abusers, some rape victims become rapists and some tortured people become torturers, but colonized nations become colonizers. Oppressed people become oppressors if they accede to power without healing their own wounds.

As other colonial societies, the North American society was established on some assumptions rarely discussed: the *primacy of the invading race, culture and religion.* Columbus assumed that certitude. That the Founding Fathers established the same assumptions on the new Promised Land a century and a half later is not surprising. Moreover, having come from countries unable to feed everyone, these idealistic colonizers saw the development of virgin lands as a sacred mission from God. They worked hard at providing sufficient food, and their divine mission promoted a material vision of development. On the same ships with the idealistic colonizers and missionaries came traders who used the same noble language for money-making purposes; they clothed their search for wealth with biblical motivations and pious proclamations.

North America's colonial past coincided with the manufacturing and capitalistic growth in Great Britain. The need for goods was important. When the new territories constrained the British to mind their own business and let the colonies become independent, the secession brought a political revolution, the birth of a republic, but not a social and cultural revolution. **The political structures changed, but the bases of their new culture were not challenged:** *primacy of the invading culture, race and religion—material development—and profit at any price.* **These remained, and gave shape to the culture of this independent country.**[45] These three ubiquitous realities of the American Way of Life, suggest that they are the main values animating its life and culture. Obedience to God, liberty, pursuit of happiness, and other proclaimed cultural values, bent by profit-making, now carry little weight in the nation's daily choices, in its diverse social structures, in its media's messages, and even in its individual citizens' choices. The oppression of the American Way of Life upon people of other countries has to be recognized. Material development and high profit are carried out at the expense of many people on every continent of the globe. A culture that promotes hyper-consumption and a structure of waste can do it only if raw materials, export crops, and cheap labor are obtained every day. Threats and pressure, psychological or military, are exercised as needed for this outcome. It is sad to remember that in Guatemala the democratic government established in 1944 as a result of a nonviolent revolution was toppled in 1954 and replaced by a dictatorship with the collusion of the C.I.A. and a banana corporation.

Messianism and the Number One Complex

The "sacred mission" that religious colonizers thought was theirs reinforced a culture of material development and profit at any price. Another consequence of this Messianism is the conviction that the country needs to be a leader and should be "Number One" in power. Official discourses, and newspaper editorials express that conviction day after day.

With a great amazement I learned that in the first decades of European settlements in New England, the colonizers were convinced that they were creating a new society better than any other that had existed before. I am still puzzled at the mind set of people landing on what they thought was a Promised Land and feeling they had a divine mission. "It was idealistic, self-denying, hopeful of divine favor for national aspirations."[46] A good example is the words of John Winthrop to his fellow passengers about to land in New England, "We must consider that we shall be as a city upon a hill, the eyes of all people are upon us; so that if we shall deal falsely with our god in this work we have undertaken and so cause him to withdraw his present help from us, we shall be made a story and a by-word through the world."[47]

This initial certitude of a mission to "realize the ancient biblical hope of a just and compassionate society" did not erode in the following generations, and Messianism became part of the North American psyche. The country has the divine role to be the model republic and to improve the state of the world, especially as defender of democracy and liberty. The belief that the U.S.A. is **a true democracy, and is the freest and best institution in the world reinforced this mission.** As many foreigners do, I recognize many wonderful aspects of the American democracy and society, and I am grateful to benefit from them. But I am far from adopting the belief that a true democracy, and the freest country in the world are here. I can love this country, admire its inhabitants, and find that some institutions are remarkable without needing to make of the U.S.A. a mandatory Number One invested with a divine mission. President Ronald Reagan encouraged a revival of the theme of the best democracy that pervaded during past centuries. The crumbling of the European communist block brought up rapturous discourses, now dampened as some Eastern European countries look to their communist past with envy. Where does this certitude about being a chosen people with a unique role come from? According to some authors, the main root of this certitude came from the Puritan's adherence to Calvin's theory of predestination. Whatever the foundation, there was and is the understanding that everything could be new, that the colonized land was empty and belonged to those who planted their flag on it.

The colonizer's Messianism might not have been shared by those who came for commercial goals, but the idealist vocabulary marked everyone. Everyone accepted these religious statements even from the cunning lips of the most crooked people. On the foundation of this messianic role, helped by the territory's immensity and vast resources, grew a strange need to be **Number One,** or to estimate everything in terms of competition. Such competitive thinking, according to psychologists, is very destructive; comparison damages relationships as it erases the uniqueness of a person or a group and competition destroys communitarian spirit as it opposes the natural law of human interdependence. People lose the ability to think of themselves as part of a larger group. A healthy desire to win evolves easily into a desire for domination or the disguised reality of it. Friends from Bolivia insisted that this competitive mentality contradicts the values of the Latin American world.

Foreigners arriving in the U.S.A. are struck by so many proclamations of being #1 in any area; to have the biggest, the largest, the tallest of anything. "We are the best" proclaimed universities, corporations, and sport teams. Seldom is that proclamation substantiated; frequently it is not even checked. It would be a laughing matter if such a need to be Number One did not bring with it violences and injustices.

In Las Vegas casinos struggle to be the largest. For a long time there were casinos with 2,500 rooms, then came one with 3,000. When two 4,000 room casinos opened it was announced that another one with 5,009 rooms would be built, the largest in the world. In another part of the world however, a 6,000 room hotel was inaugurated. Not to be outdone, another company announced several buildings will total a higher number on the same piece of land. Size is what is important, not the quality of the accommodations. Nobody questions how the employees will feel in such a monstrous hotel. The desire to be Number One in number of rooms, and to use that reference for publicity continues to be the leading factor.

Much of the desire to be Number One is clearly nationalistic. Understandably individuals and nations want to excel, but this desire can be distorted into the search for mastery over others. In the corporate field, as in the international field, the desire for total supremacy is obvious. The Number One syndrome, often associated with the wish for unchallenged military power, gives total superiority and domination in both the military and economic domains.[48]

My country of origin, France, suffered over a few centuries from a similar Number one complex, though its origins were quite different. For a long time France's population was between 30% and 50% of Europe's population, providing France with a strong army that engaged in many wars. Now the French people are not that proud of the violences done to other countries.

Most likely the present North American culture bears additional scars from the colonial period. The ones mentioned seem to have the greatest continuous role in fostering violence in the present culture. With the first settlers, even the best intentioned, came the oppression of the Natives; then the need of labor for agricultural development made slavery acceptable. Shortly after establishing the first settlements authorities in England made sure that the colonists obeyed London and paid their dues and taxes. Political independence was gained and was celebrated. It is difficult for citizens of any independent country to look at their colonial past. Proud of their liberation from British domination, few American citizens accept even the hypothesis of colonial scars subsisting in the mentality or in the structures of their nation. To a messianic nation, they think, God surely avoided wounds and mistakes!

I am continuously amazed by the total lack of reference to the colonial past of the U.S.A. Is it an amnesia? Is it a shame to have been a colony? Some people seem to remember history (and so little!) only after the ringing of Liberty Bell. During my six years in Chicago I lived with midwesterners and New Englanders. The first century and a half of their forefathers seemed to have been erased by the Declaration of Independence. This reaction baffles me. The territory of France was a Roman colony, and this brings pride. The Romans left amazing buildings and roads. They also left a less suitable heritage: centralism, legalism, etc. The British heritage did not include only taxes; it included a language, a religion, and an exceptionally good judicial system. Why is there so deep a wound in the North American psyche? Whatever the reasons, no healing of these old wounds will happen without a national upsurge of truth and courage.

Are Americans ready to look at their colonial past, to face the weight of the principles that were imposed by the traders on their forefathers, and to exorcise the evil out of these principles? Will they dare to have a critical mind towards them? **If not, I am afraid that racism, disdain for others, and total submission to a materialistic vision of development and profit-making will be brought to the level of a practiced civil religion.[49] A clear result will be the growing of violence and discrimination against minorities, the arrogance toward a life milieu and the destruction of it when so-called development or a greedy search for profit is at stake.** This critical look at the past may be feared by most U.S. citizens. Those who benefit from the domination of the materialistic values will resist such a process of critique. Nevertheless, I feel more and more that the beginning of a collective psychoanalysis could bring healing to many violences from which we all suffer. It is in the hands of grass roots groups to initiate and develop the process of facing the reality and eliminating the poison that makes the North American culture so unhealthy for its own members, and for the whole earth. It is a gigantic task, but not impossible for a nation so rich in human resources and with such a past.

Questions for Reflection

- What do you feel is most important in this chapter?

- What struck you in this chapter? How do you deal with your feelings about these observations?

- What deep patterns do you think the colonial past has left in the culture? What seems to you the most conducive to violence?

- How can we come to the realization of a national psychotherapy that can heal the birth wounds of the North American culture?

- In a culture which undervalues history, and invites people to run towards any kind of future, how can we find healing from the scars of the colonial era, its worship of material prosperity, its racism, its Messianism, its "number one" syndrome, its imperialist spirit?

CHAPTER FIVE

Individual and National Dreams

The American Dream of the Individual

FOR THE INDIVIDUAL the American dream is a complex reality that includes freedom of religion, of speech, and of behavior. It imagines all as equals, able to participate in the same democracy, capable to acceding to the highest charges and responsibilities, free from oppression and exploitation. At the same time each one should have access to wealth, own a house, and prepare a future for the children. The market culture has twisted the American dream; the former realities are still mentioned but with a different meaning, and the dream is reduced to the accumulation of material possessions.

Shortly after my arrival in Chicago in 1973, before working as a day laborer, I applied for some steady jobs. One interviewer, surprised by someone coming from France, warned me, "This country is no longer a place where the streets are paved with gold. It is hard to make a living." Now Las Vegas seems like the final place in the U.S.A. where money comes by the pail-full—at least by big plastic containers—as you play the slot machines. The casinos owe their prosperity to the dreams of the gamblers. After their money falls into the hands of the casinos owners, like into a deep

81

ravine, gamblers are forced to face the reality of their life which stays the same or becomes worse. Their dream is still on the other side of the ravine.[50] Along with those who come to Las Vegas hoping for the miracle of becoming rich overnight, come some homeless who long for relief from their distressing situation, and maybe to become rich. Everyone has heard of someone who knows someone who knows someone who hit a big win. True or false, it fuels the dreams and exacerbates the desires. Why not me? The kingdom of illusion is everywhere—fake gold on the building facades, fake grandiosity, fake historical places—making it more difficult to see the difference between reality, illusion and dream. Destitutes, poor, and people of modest means are submitted to the obscene display of money; of easy win; of lavish spending; of enticement to spend more. Their lack of financial means becomes more painful. Frustrations brew and accumulate. Despair, suicide, violence of various types, and social explosions can happen at any time.

Frustrated dreams are not new to America. The tremendous possibilities of a large territory amazed me as they had astounded many generations of immigrants. They saw a rich land, apparently unlimited natural resources, and immediate material prosperity. The most extravagant dreams could be fulfilled if you were courageous and held yourself by the bootstraps. During three and half centuries, a myth grew, and the American dream took shape. On the steps of the British merchants and their colonial proxies, the market society became the backbone of the new country and continued to develop its potentialities in unpredictable growth, giving reality to some material dreams.

Throughout two centuries a few enterprising immigrants who arrived poor realized the American dream. The promise in the Declaration of Independence, *Life, Liberty, and the Pursuit of Happiness,* became true for them. Arriving with a few coins in their pockets, they prospered; some even became outrageously affluent. I know someone who arrived in California twenty years ago with $50. One year later he had $12 million, earned lawfully in the stock market. Today people harvest big profits not only by millions but by billions. A few similar stories reinforce the myth that everyone can quickly become rich: "From rags to riches." Recently, Ted Turner discovered that in one year his fortune had grown by one billion, and he decided to give this billion to the United Nations. Bill Gates is now worth more than 33 billion!

In the post World War II era the colossal industrial structure which had been developed for the war's victory needed to find outlets for its gigantic production. Simultaneously a larger part of the population acceded to more affluence. Within such a context and in keeping with the patterns of liberal economics, the marketing strategy directed its efforts towards creating new desires in order to sell the excess of goods. The immediate satisfaction of wants, which before seemed unrealistic, became accessible to the middle class. New waves of wants swept over potential consumers. Why wait when immediate satisfaction was offered so easily? *Wants* took the place of *needs,* and this immediate satisfaction or instant gratification was not only welcomed, but also presented as a true cultural value. **It became part of the American Way of Life to satisfy immediately any *want,* as abundance allowed.**

Credit becomes a must and accelerates the immediacy of satisfaction. "Quick" and "now" are key words in this time aspect of the culture. Each one of us received dozens of unsolicited credit cards. Whoever, like me, does not have a credit card is handicapped and almost suspected as a criminal. In the present situation many people get frustrated if there is not satisfaction and in fact a quick, immediate satisfaction of their wants, even those far remote from their needs. Adults are not the only ones to be subject to this transformation: In the last three decades children were systematically allured to increase and satisfy their wants. Before these last years the training of children emphasized the fulfillment of their needs through effort, learning and saving. Now both youth and adults ignore that preparation, get frustrated if their wants are not satisfied immediately, and become violent.

The American dream became a golden reality for a few around whose tales and legends became widespread and exaggerated. A sizable middle class experienced a more modest success. However, for a growing number during the last twenty years the dream of a steady job, a house, education for the children, and life in a society of equals remained remote—still a dream, surrounded by fog.[51] From this foggy dream the Sirens continue to allure, but prudishly they avoid being seen! "Maybe it will be for our children," said resigned and frugal people working hard to send their children to college. As adults, many of these children remain unemployed.

Similarly, poor people living in slums and conditioned by advertising, dream of a good life like that seen in movies or on television. They want to imitate the clothing of their heroes, their eating and drinking habits, their furniture and even their gadgets. With such a set of desires, people become extremely vulnerable to persuasive salespersons or telemarketers. Temporarily credit resolves the situation, but debts add up and burdens become unbearable. One after the other, the stories that I hear are the same. Frustrations and anger easily lead to violence, a violence that becomes casual, like a routine, or the mob violence and the rioting. Politicians and the media then express surprise, because they did not pay attention to the many causes leading to frustration. A consumer driven society systematically arousing people's wants exacerbates the frustrations of those whose desire for material gratification far exceeds their resources. In becoming more acute their desires create a critical situation.

The circulation of U.S. films and television programs all over the world collaborates actively in developing a profusion of unrealistic wants within poorer countries. Frustration at being deprived of many amenities follows quickly and gives rise to envy and anger. Within indigenous cultures those who want to keep their traditional way of life conflict with promoters of the American Way who pretend that such amenities are necessary for the future of their people.

Psychologists show how addictions enslave people. Throughout centuries, moralists of various cultures understood this human dynamic and called addictions by other names: passions, sinful tendencies, darkness. What is new in our society is the growing number of people moving from one dependency to another. I saw many who had struggled successfully against their alcohol dependency, fall into drug, gambling or sex addiction. A reason seems to be that our North American culture causes a great many wounds of relationships and of frustrated wants. Giving in to an addiction may temporarily release the tension created by the injuries. People believe it will heal or at least numb their wounds, when the truth is that it creates a dependency widening and deepening these. Lighting a cigarette, then another one, drinking a glass of alcohol, then another, is frequently done to relieve the stress, the loneliness, the doubt about one's own worth. Drug addiction, gambling addiction, sexual addiction, power addiction and now shopping addiction follow the same pattern.

Addicted people depend more and more on the object of their want, which becomes a need. When they lack it, their frustration can be so strong that reason, love and justice have little bearing on their behavior. Lies, cheatings, robberies and physical violence which can go as far as murder are often the byproduct of such intense desire to fulfill their tendency or numb their feeling of guilt. In Las Vegas for a few years two of our neighbors were drug dealers. We have first hand experience how wild the dealers' clients can be when they are in need of their drug, and how creative they are for stealing! Drug dealers use guns against those who did not pay, the rival gangs, and people who informed the police. Compulsive buyers often place their families in a distressing situation. Not all of them have the means of Imelda Marcos, well known for her hundreds of shoes. Poverty can coexist with and be the result of a house full of objects; these did not extinguish the intensity of the feeling of void, and the desire for more things.

The myth of the American dream accessible to everyone did not materialize for a sizable minority. The Constitution and Declaration of Independence made promises that everyone learns at school. The market culture reduced the dream to only becoming rich. To promise to every American richness is in itself a violence towards the rest of the planet, as it can be done only at the expense of others. When that promise is not held, disappointment grows. In the last decades this has led to an accumulation of personal, racial, regional and class frustrations.

The Manifest Destiny of the Nation

Furthermore, the country as a whole bears the consequences of a collective dream presented as a messianic mission, whose existence brings tragic and unexpected violence. From time to time, politicians and church leaders refer to that very ambiguous *manifest destiny*. I pointed out in a previous chapter how that notion nurtured the "Number One" complex so anchored in the North American psyche. Nobody asks, "Who gave that mission? How was it given? What is the exact mission? What were the successive understandings of that mission?" And now that it seems the mission has not been fulfilled, does the common psyche of the North American people bear a wound of this failure?

I came from a country that has been called the *Oldest daughter of the Church* (the Roman Catholic Church). That title was received in the 8th century after the French King helped a Pope obtain a territory in order to give the papacy physical independence from other powers. Later, this title taken out of its original context became very damaging to the spirit of the French Catholics. It gave birth to an excessive religious pride and arrogance. How I wish that Americans would not fall into the same arrogance!

The first settlers' understanding of their divine mission continues to weigh dramatically on the North American mentality and culture. I will not elaborate on past actions like the massacres of Native Americans and the violation of the treaties with them, or the rivalry with other colonists supposedly not invested by God for a similar mission. Right now the spreading of the American Way of Life over all the continents is still fueled by a missionary zeal that is contaminated by the commercial greed. It is sometimes difficult to know what true motivations give birth to the zealous activity. "We have the best democracy in the world, we have the best economic system, we need to bring liberty to people—it is our Mission," are a few statements heard quite often, but seldom challenged! How is it that many North Americans still believe that every inhabitant of our planet could adopt the American Way of Life? Economists have demonstrated that this Way of Life is too lavish and not sustainable with the limited resources of the planet. Moreover, some civilizations proclaim clearly that they do not want such a Way of Life, which will destroy the meaning of their existence. Stubbornly, many people around me continue to think as if it were possible. "**We have to spread our system and our culture! It is a divine mission!**" The behavior of various religious groups and sects from the U.S.A. living in foreign countries stems from this certitude that the American nation has a manifest destiny. The CIA exploited this ambiguous religious and nationalistic missionary zeal, especially in Venezuela and other Latin American countries. Violences followed. The 1991 Gulf war's crusade for liberty obscenely covered up less generous motivations. Unfortunately, other recent examples abound. The impact that such themes have on public opinion is without doubt very strong even when people question the sincerity of those who use these topics.

I believe that it is time for the U.S.A. as a whole to look clearly at that mission and to face its ambiguities and its resulting violence. A collective national psychotherapy is urgently needed. It would help to heal an arrogance that the enormous material power of the United States continuously nurtures. A courageous process is needed to bring the profound healing which is required. Will there be political or religious leaders giving impetus to such a task?

This messianic mission is very much connected to the prevalent American image of God. I am not sure that many

North Americans realize how their understanding of God arose more from a limited part of the Old Testament than from the New Testament. This statement shocked good friends of mine, who afterwards came to agree with me. Even after twenty-five years in contact with religious milieus, it amazes me to observe how that old image prevails. In early Hebrew history the chosen people understood that their fidelity was associated with their material prosperity. The Hebrews of old might have needed such a material sign to teach them that God cared for the spiritual mission they received. By his teaching, his whole life, and his catastrophic end, Jesus was a scandal for the Jews of his time; a material and psychological failure! This terminated the era of God-giver-of-riches and warrantor of material prosperity that the prophets had challenged to no avail. Nevertheless, two millennia later the unholy alliance of God and money is still illustrated by the motto *In God we Trust* written on U.S. currency only a few decades ago! The weakest and the most vulnerable were victims of violence in order to reach the prosperity supposed to be the "will of God". These victims of violence are the Native Americans, Afro-Americans, the poor who did not make it, and Third World countries depleted of their resources and whose underpaid labor force brought prosperity to the economy of the world leader.

How did it happen that North American's faith in God came to be dominated by this vision inherited from the beginning of the Old Testament? The consequences are dramatic for the Christian faith and for social life. Following Max Weber,[52] many social observers credit the Puritans, who grew in the Calvinist theology, for this understanding. For them the sign of predestined persons was their material success. Today the majority of the Churches, even of Calvinist background, are critical of that explanation, but their position does not prevent Churches with the maxim "be rich, be happy" from being enthusiastically followed. These groups harmonize with the dominant mentality shaping the culture, which continues to associate wealth with God's blessing or even with God's predestination. The Old Testament blessing manifested in material goods was easier to listen to and overpowered Jesus Christ's critique of wealth. I encountered examples of that prevalent mentality in my day labor companions or in many homeless persons. Because they are poor and did not make it, they believe they are rejected by God. Society tells them again and again that this is truly the reason for their poverty. Public policies and regulations reinforce this explanation.

In contrast to the European churches, the North American churches have not had their idea of God as author and defender of wealth challenged by the Marxist critique. This historical fact is of considerable importance, and most Americans do not realize what purification of their Christian faith could have resulted from such a confrontation. The fear of receiving such a critique from outsiders of the faith community, and especially from Marxism, makes it more urgent to develop an inner critique which requires historical and scriptural data. The responsibility of believers to prevent wealthy people from imposing on the churches an ethic and a theological reasoning divorced from the base of their faith is tremendous and urgent.

In a parallel manner I am surprised that in this country, where psychologists are at every corner and psychology developed so many trends, it is a rarity when depth psychology critiques the prevalent cultural vision of God: God-the-tranquilizer, God-the-broker, God-the-insurance-agent. Jesus Christ has turned upside down such a vision by his life and his teaching. Similarly he erased the idea of a God showing favoritism and inviting competition. God is tender towards every human. God is a compassionate God. From time to time Peace Churches, theologians, spiritual leaders, or saintly figures like Dorothy Day have attempted to challenge the vision prevalent in the culture, but the public opinion has not followed this critique, and continues to feel comfortable with a truncated understanding of the Old Testament. The lack of self-critique of our relationships with God is not a private question involving only individual faith. Its consequences are huge in nurturing violences brought by the culture we live in. Believers have here a very important challenge. Will we pick up the gauntlet?

Moreover, I see signs of a deep frustration that the exceptional mission that has been dreamt of remains unrealized. A set of violences is brought by this disappointment. Inside the U.S.A. there is the realization that the nation is moving in the opposite direction of what the Founding Fathers had dreamed, and that might have been partly realized during the American history. Various studies have been done on this topic.[53] The Promised Land does not host the expected New Society, where people are equal, free from oppressions and exploitations, and have equal opportunity. Freedom is shrinking. The primary freedom, to make profit and accrue wealth, is held by the few. A class society is becoming compartmentalized with little possibility of entering the castes of the most privileged. Some people, especially the homeless, feel they are considered less valuable than the pets of many. They are considered as commodities.

To these disillusions on the internal level, there is a national frustration that the manifest destiny of the American people is not recognized by everyone on this planet. This not only wounds the pride, but brings a crisis at a religious level. It shakes the belief in God's predilection for America and shows the extent of the realm of evil. I have been amazed how these topics become so present in every international crisis that I witnessed during the last 25 years. People are frustrated that the divine mission has not been fulfilled as they have dreamed. Easily accepted by public opinion, national bursts of violence against whoever resists the "benevolence" and the "divine" nature of the U.S.A. international policy, might be the result of the wound left by this unrealized mission. This national frustration, which can be compared to the individual frustration of those who did not reach the American dream, is rarely questioned and analyzed. This is not surprising, as the indiscreet and irreverent questions that I formulated above about the origin of the mission still seem to be avoided.

With the eyes of a foreigner, I see an incredible violence in the belief in a Manifest Destiny. I see also the wounds inside North Americans that this exceptional mission has not been realized as they have dreamed. More violence follows.

Questions for Reflection

- *What do you feel is important in this last chapter?*

- *What is stirred in you by this chapter?*

- *What are your dreams concerning your personal future?*

- *What are your dreams concerning the national future?*

- *What other role models, and other processes have you experienced and were more gratifying than instant gratification? How can we foster these?*

- *Can you think of recent examples of the theme of "manifest destiny" brought by the media, politicians or church people?*

- *How can a psychotherapy of the "mission of the USA" begin and bring healing?*

CHAPTER SIX

An Individualistic Role Model, the "Self-made Man"

The Self-made Man,[54]
Model of a Particular Individualism

WHEN I ARRIVED IN THIS COUNTRY, some of my brothers warned me about American individualism and its many manifestations. I laughed and said, "It is not possible to be more individualistic than French people!" "You will see!" answered my companions, "We Americans really **are** individualists." Day after day the differences between French and North American individualism became clearer. These differences are aptly illustrated in two caricatures. The French cartoon involves the two legendary personages from the South of France, Marius and Olive. They have had an argument about politics. It is well known that in France there are as many political parties as there are voters, and each "head of a political party" is passionate! So, at the end of their argument, Marius solemnly said to Olive, "Olive, our relationship is finished; between us it is broken forever; I swear that I will not see you anymore!" Marius takes a breath, walks a few steps, then says: "Let us go to the *bistro* and have a drink together." The American cartoon represents a pioneer, potential settler, riding to the West; in the middle of the Plains, he stops his horse, puts a stick into the ground, takes his gun into his hands and declares, "From that spot of mine, if I see anyone walking on my property, I will shoot him." The French individualism kept a strong communitarian dimension while the American model did not. On the contrary the sociologist Robert Bellah, in his book *Habits of the Heart, Individualism and Commitment in American Life,* writes "Individualism lies at the very core of American culture"[55] and adds that even people who work for the community do so in an individualistic way. He mentions four traditions of individualism: a biblical individualism, a civic individualism, and two manifestations of the modern individualism, a utilitarian and an expressive individualism.

Referring to Tocqueville who "described the American individualism . . . with a mixture of admiration and anxiety," Bellah continues "it seems to us that it is individualism, and not equality, as Tocqueville thought, that has marched inexorably through our history. We are concerned that this individualism may have grown cancerous—that it may be destroying those social integuments that Tocqueville saw as moderating its more destructive potentialities, that it may be threatening to the survival of freedom itself."[56]

Bellah's team did a rigorous and thorough study of American individualism; they were careful not to equate it with self-centeredness. After this landmark work all that I could say in these short pages about a few personal events and encounters would seem superficial. I want to center my reflections around a model of a particular individualism—the self-made man—which seems to me the most important for my exploration of the relationships between culture and violence. I will not report events concerning the many self-made men I encountered, as it is touchy to be too specific about people who are not successful self-made men, but inherited the individualism attached to this model. They are incomplete persons whose development has been blocked. Sadly, even in persons committed to religious community life I have encountered self-made men. They do not yet realize that their wholeness depends upon their acceptance of nurturing relationships, not upon the relinquishment of responsibility and accountability to their community, humankind, and creation. My search for the cultural values and principles conducive to violence leads me to a deeper reflection on the self-made man, to better understand if and why that role model creates various violences. The Catholic comprehension of the human person clarifies this point for me. Therefore, this chapter will borrow from anthropological reflections tied to both psychology and philosophy. My thesis is that the self-made man is an underdeveloped wounded person and that his woundedness provokes frustrations and violences.

The police, the media, your neighbors, and maybe you yourself point fingers at gang members. How many people are aware that the wounds of the self-made teen-ager are partly healed through belonging to a gang where he can develop relationships of confidence and responsibility? My friends who are street educators know well that aspect of the gang phenomenon. At the other end of the success scale, how many successful business persons are lonely as Howard Hughes, or have broken families? It might be easier to build a financial empire than to be related to a wife and children who require constant listening and attentiveness. Those who are familiar with the texts of the New Testament remember that in the first Epistle to the Corinthians, Paul of Tarsus warns of the danger of doing great things, and not having love that is the core of human existence.[57] It is amazing how often people try to do a repair job by themselves without looking at the book or the manual they have laid aside. "It is a challenge, and I am able to do it" is what I often hear. Following that proud proclamation I have witnessed many failures!

The *self-made man* is a role model for many North Americans. Since the first Europeans settled on the continent, North Americans have celebrated the qualities of determination, courage and the cleverness of people coming from humble backgrounds who have attained envied positions. Special honor and heroic status are reserved for those who, with limited education, training, or financial resources, have attained the American Dream with their sweat and endurance. The self-made man is the American success story.

Without doubt the one who is eager to become a self-made man develops qualities and gifts which otherwise might have remained dormant. His determination mobilizes his own energies and has a contagious effect on others who follow his example. He might be an undisciplined student at school, but for the knowledge he wants to acquire by himself he self-imposes a strict and fruitful discipline. Frequently, the results of his actions are not only beneficial to himself but serve the society. Persons who otherwise would have remained hidden and unused because of the distraction or the contempt of others are encouraged by the self-made model to accede to high responsibilities.

On the other hand, when the self-made man expresses pride in having achieved success on his own he damages his ability to become fully human. "No one gave me anything," he says. "I did it on my own. Why can't they? Instead of looking for a hand-out, people should do what I did. I started from nothing. I did it by myself." The pioneering, immigrant spirit is often alluded to by self-made men. In recent years President Ronald Reagan gave a new glow to this role model calling for a return to the pioneer qualities.

While the successful self-made man holds a position of esteem in society other self-made men, in adverse circum-stances crumble from lofty positions and are bitter. In counse-lors' waiting rooms, they meet others who struggle with the pain of failure, unable to fulfill the dream, unable to make it on their own. The pride on which their self-worth was based is shattered. In this competitive world there is no pity for those who don't make it: the weak, the unadapted, and those who, for one reason or another, did not keep up their guard.

The mythical role of the self-made man raises questions for the successful and unsuccessful alike. What does the model of the self-made man say about what it means to be human? How does one become a complete person? Is the ideal human being independent of others?

Critics from a variety of disciplines have addressed these questions. Social commentators and ethicists denounce the destructiveness of North American individualism. Similarly, scholars as well as community organizers lament the lack of communitarian spirit essential for a healthy society. Counse-lors see their clients' relationships with family and friends as crucial for personal well-being.

From a spiritual perspective rooted in the Christian gos-pel vision, I understand four relationships are essential for becoming fully human:

1. Relationships with other persons and groups, small or large.

2. Relationship with God.

3. Relationship with all of creation, animate and inani-mate.

4. Relationship with the totality of the self, including the "dark" or "shadow" parts.

This understanding of what it means to be human is in tension with the assumptions of the model of the self-made man. In contrast to the self-made man's sense of self-sufficiency and pride of self-achievement, the spiritual understanding is that a person becomes truly human only in the process of being in relationships of integrity at these four levels. The Christian vision is that a person is created through relationships.[58] Growing as a person means entering fully into these relationships and being changed by them. The Trinity is the ideal community of persons. In the Judeo-Christian tradition human beings created "in God's image" enter into their own reality only when they follow God into that life of relationships. Into this life-giving relationship Christ invites humans to move, and to bring with them the whole of Creation.

Let us now examine each of these relationships.

1. Interpersonal relationships. Relationships between persons can be transforming, making life more whole. Healthy relationships bring life as one is recognized worthy of attention, worthy of being listened to, worthy of genuine respect. This becomes even more vital in a society where people often are considered objects or commodities. Good relationships awaken a sense of worth and develop confidence and mutual respect. Frequently these beneficial effects are experienced at work or in the neighborhood. Good relationships with co-workers, the boss, or neighbors are constructive. Likewise bad relationships are destructive; they not only make life miserable, but can shake and destroy the personality. Furthermore, relationships of deep friendship, affection and love may free persons to release and share gifts buried within. Similarly, they offer a more realistic view of one's limitations. Persons who are genuinely loved blossom in amazing ways. When people discover that they are able to love and to fulfill responsibilities in relationships, they feel complete, less alone, closer to their true self. What a treasure it is to have authentic intimate friends! Those fortunate enough to have loving parents and siblings experience how shared love contributes to their wholeness.

Experiencing the dignity of the self and the other, sensing the sacred in the self and the other, seeing the divine within the self and the other are essential for true human relationships. If one is casual with the treasure within oneself or the other, the relationship deteriorates and may break. Each one of us has a direct experience of that tragic happening. Human beings are deeply wounded by being used, manipulated or discarded. Respect and more significantly reverence are corner stones of any relationship.

Group and community relationships provide opportunities for discovering both personal limitations and unique resources. Participation in a community where members serve one another, accept mutual feedback, and support one another gives wider dimensions to life. Persons may be healed and revitalized in community. Quite often the vitality of a community is perceived most clearly after people have lost contact with that nurturing group. Persons who suffer such loss feel incomplete; they long to be relieved from inexplicable contradictions within themselves, and in the world as well. The trauma of separation, even from less intimate communities such as work or neighborhood associations, can be very dramatic, threatening life itself.

Becoming human includes the understanding that people share a common humanity and a common world. Each life impacts on all others. Failure to recognize the essential unity of all creation and failure to accept opportunities for involvement with and service in the larger community deprives persons of an indispensable element of growth, and robs society of that person's gifts. No one grows fully human without accepting responsibility for others in the same boat. These reflections illustrate the incompleteness of the self-made man. While he prides himself in his aloneness, in reality he is suffering a terrible loss.

2. *Relationship with God.* Judeo-Christian tradition proclaims that a healthy relationship with God is vital for becoming fully human. Not every self-made man recognizes the existence of God, but when he does, he often prays the prayer of the Pharisee, "Lord, I thank Thee that I am not as other men . . ." The prayer of the truly human person, on the other hand, seeks a relationship with God that accepts God as God is, and accepts himself as he is, not attempting to look better or worse than he really is. Truth is the law; pretense is not acceptable.

The truly human person recognizes God as both transcendent—unique, holy, the One from whom everything comes—and at the same time, immanent, God with us, God in us, God **the very low,**[59] God the essence and source of all love, God who desires humankind's collaboration in God's Trinity life. God initiates relationships that give dignity to all men and women.

The self-made man who participates in the creative activity of God by making himself "successful" but who denies or ignores his need for relationships of integrity with God and others is an undeveloped human. Persons become fully developed only in loving others, as God loves. The God of the Bible is not a lone "self-made Superman." The God of the Bible is not a "self-made God" impersonally manipulating creation and creatures for God's "success." The God of the Bible is a covenant community God who invites humanity to live in relationship with God and with all creation.

Persons truly related to God recognize both their sinfulness and smallness as well as their incredible richness coming from the One who is at the center of their being. Such persons grow in their humanness as they face their limits and their shadows and experience God's unconditional love. They respond to the mysterious and unavoidable invitation to love with a life that, while imperfect, keeps developing because God's strength is at its source. The self-made man, on the other hand, having created God in his own image as a far-away tyrant or someone (a buddy) to be manipulated, cannot grow into full humanity. His pride is a serious obstacle blocking self-understanding and a true relationship with the Creator.

These reflections on the relationship with God followed the reflection on the interpersonal relationships because relationship with the Mysterious One most often follows the human experience of relationship with others and is profoundly influenced by these. It is tragic that those who never experienced a positive human relationship have an image of God which contradicts the experience of the mystics of all religions. Those who have only experienced negative human relationship often see God as tyrannical, distant, angry or insensitive; those who have experienced utilitarian human relationships, frequently see God as a good helper for their success; those who have experienced some loving human relationships are more prone to enter into the mystical experience of communion, union and transformation.

3. *Relationship with all of creation, animate and inanimate.*   As a product of the economically focused culture of North

America, the self-made man sees all of creation as resources to serve his needs, wants and desires. Consistent with his views of God and other humans, the self-made man sees the non-human world as objects for his domination on the way to success. This exploitative relationship destroys the fragile equilibrium on the Earth.

Being fully human includes the awareness that humans are one part of the universe. Other creatures are our brothers and sisters needing respect and offering it. Their *raison d'être* goes beyond being commodities for the material welfare of humankind. The self-made man is in need of conversion to this understanding of inter-relatedness with all of creation. Many voices today urgently stress that humankind renounce the domination and exploitation of the Earth, and establish respectful relationships between human beings and the Cosmos. Some psychologists claim that today's ecological crisis threatening sustainable life on earth, injects fear and increases the difficulty for future planning. The domination mentality towards Creation damages the inner core of humanity; the full extent of the damage has yet to be explored. Corporations or persons who consider only the material aspect of development demonstrate this way of thinking.

4. *Relationship with the totality of the self, including the "dark" or "shadow" parts.* To become fully human one needs to develop a courageous and friendly relationship with that, not easily accepted, dark part of ourselves, one's shadow. It takes much time and impressive fortitude to recognize, to face, and to accept the shadow aspects of ourselves. We prefer to place the blame on others or on events. It is not enough to make that step of acceptance. One needs a friendly but non-complacent relationship with one's shadow. This requires cleverness, pluck, and a truly compassionate love for one's

self. One is often led to believe that this is selfish. It takes a long process to discover that this friendly relationship with one's shadow is the way God loves us. This discovery is a prerequisite for true inner peace and for deepening one's relationships with God and others. Even though St. Francis of Assisi recognized clearly that every human being has a dark side, and is a sinner, he invited his followers to develop inside themselves virtues, instead of fighting against their sins. When virtues or the light inside us grows, the dark side of us that leans towards sin decreases considerably.

The self-made person, dependent on success for his self-worth, cannot acknowledge his shadow. His pride blocks his need for God or others. Barring himself from true relatedness, he is a prisoner in his own self-made cell, a wounded man. He has lost touch with the core of his humanness, and thus with his divineness.

The model of the self-made man must crumble. To liberate the self-made man captive in his self-made illusions, we must remove him from his pedestal. Otherwise many more will self-make themselves into disintegration. In doing so they will bring the universe to the brink of destruction. Often the self-made man does not appear threatening, but behind the smile of his auto-satisfaction lies a terrible violence that has destroyed his best potential to become fully human. The convulsions of that auto-destruction have far-reaching repercussions, especially if he is a powerful person.

Freeing the self-made man from his prison pedestal will be a very difficult enterprise. Self-made men are blocked in their liberation by the general admiration they receive. Setting them up as role models needs to be reconsidered. There are other models. Impressive among alternative models is the

Christian model that cultivates the four types of relationships discussed above. Persons who integrate this model bring life-giving ripples in the deserts of our lives and our world. Such persons recognize that they owe much to many. Being more unified within themselves, they become community builders giving to and receiving from others. Their wholeness is full of promise for others and for all creation. The masculine and the feminine in them are unified, or some people would say their animus and their anima are at peace with each other. In the process of integrating all their potentialities and their gifts, they are truly the peacemakers.

Why would anyone choose to remain a self-made larva of a person instead of becoming a whole human being? Self-made men, seduced by the self-made-model and blinded by their own success, are not condemned to stay forever in their undeveloped stage. They may also become human if they give up their pride and dominating spirit to enter respectful relationships. The whole Creation awaits the metamorphosis of the self-made man into a fully human being. When this happens many relationships will be restored and many violences will evanesce.

Self-service: Is It Innocuous?

Another aspect of individualism that I encounter every day is expressed and developed by the quasi-national institution of the **self-service**. I dare to mention it even though it is a "holy cow" of the contemporary culture. Everyone knows the many advantages of self-service. It is convenient in many respects. It allows each one to one's own choice. Nevertheless, are we attached to it because it saves us the effort to relate to persons with their own personalities and weaknesses? To deal with an automatic machine might be less frustrating (at least if the machine works!) than to face an overworked and angry employee.

But are we not the losers by opting for the easy way out? Did you ever compare a common meal around a table, food circulating from one to the other, with a self-service meal where most of the people feel excused from attentiveness to the needs of their neighbors? Friends raised inside other cultures have told me how difficult it was for them to adapt to the "parties", at least those on the West Coast. "Help yourself. Feel at home" are the magic words of welcome; then if people are too shy to go ahead, even to the cooler, they can stay thirsty or starve. I know some Hispanics, Asians or Europeans who, frustrated, quickly left a party, and I deeply sympathize with them. Even after twenty-five years I am uncomfortable with what I feel to be discourteous. Fortunately, some hosts and some guests alike are able to associate the informality of a self-service meal with a tactful attention to all the company. We encounter this self-service mentality in all the aspects of the family life, "Why would I watch the same TV program that pleases the whole family? or the group? I need my individual TV." Then the family becomes a juxtaposition of persons parallel to each other, not encountering each other. "Do your things. Let me do my things." That behavior is considerably helped by self-service.

Fast food restaurants appear everywhere, even in our poor neighborhood. Surely it is useful for people in a hurry and with limited income. However, looking at some of the fast food counters the image that often comes to my mind is a stable with stalls, and horses eating their hay side by side. A distressing vision of a society! Not the convivial model with listening and interactions!

Similarly several groups and parishes complain about the self-service mentality of their constituency: some members do not feel connected to other members of the community. This partition inside groups or communities is unfortunately true at all levels of the North American social fabric. Unions and political parties too complain of that consumer, self-service attitude towards their organization. The often quoted sentence of J.F. Kennedy reminds us that self-centered individualism is ready to penetrate in our soul, "Ask not what your country can do for you; ask what you can do for your country."

Self-service erodes attentiveness to others more than people realize, it brings a true violence towards the relationships inside a community, a group, a family, letting self-centeredness contaminate the ties. For a time self-service was a convenient way of doing. Now it has expanded its domain in so many areas of our life that it has become an important part of the culture. We have here one more example of old cultural values replaced subtly by what at first appeared only an easier way of doing. Self-service is related to the self-made man mentality and contributes to the violence surrounding us.

The Truncated Anthropology of the Self-made Man, a Cause of Violence

In the preceding pages I briefly described the self-made man, and the violence he inflicts on himself, thus worsening his traumas. This situation arises when a human being aims at self-sufficiency and takes pride in it. In reality it damages him and impedes his growth.

The role model of the self-made man, and to a lesser extent the self-service mentality and structures, are immediate causes of violence; they are the trunk of the tree of violence, not the roots. It may be beneficial to reflect, even briefly, on the deeper causes, the roots of these manifestations of North American individualism.

How did the self-made man notion develop and why does it continue to be an important role-model shaping the behavior of millions of persons? This icon of American life continues to puzzle me. I think it can be explained accurately in the following manner. Newcomers on the American continent needed to work hard and struggle against a nature almost virgin. They could not count on relatives who remained in the "old countries." Moreover, before their departure from Europe many had been wounded by dysfunctional communitarian structures. In their countries of origin, the first colonizers had suffered oppression from enemy armies or soldiers of their own country, from authoritarian regimes, or from intolerant persecuting Churches. The frequent alliance of Church and State showed them the destructive consequences of groups, communities, or nations. They and their loved ones had been victims. Very likely the anthropology enfleshed by the self-made man grew from the struggle for life and from the wounds of past dysfunctional relationships. Furthermore, the Calvinist anthropology nurturing the early colonizers encouraged individualism, even though the new settlers often lived in close communities. Whatever the exact reasons, the immigrants of the first decades seem to have developed a distorted vision of the human being: The self-made man was quickly placed on a pedestal. This situation made it difficult for them to understand that **an individual needs to accept the challenge of being part of communities in order to grow.** This remark does not apply to some exceptional but small communities especially found in the Peace Churches: Mennonites, Hutterites, Church of the Brethren, Amish, and Quakers, whose commitment to community life for fidelity to the Gospel is striking. Tocqueville's amazement in seeing the multitude of associations and groups[60] does not seem to contradict these remarks on the individualist model of the self-made man. Some authors have pointed out that the need for the warmth or the security offered by a group might have favored the creation of associations. These two utilitarian purposes are different from accepting participation in a challenging community in order to grow.

The maturation of the person requires communities of various sizes. Each one offers a unique challenge needed for wholeness. The challenge of the couple and the family is different from that of the nation. Everybody needs to face most of these challenges. To refuse the limitations accompanying the commitment to a group or community life handicaps the development of the individual and damages one's hope of becoming a whole person.[61]

My statement that the current anthropology is truncated and is the main cause of violence of the North American culture may provoke skepticism and raise eyebrows. Few people address this aspect of the North American culture. More sensitive to it than most other cultural critics, because my youth was nurtured by a different culture, I came to this country when almost fifty years of age. Furthermore, it is usual for people to deny a hereditary reality, even when one's own actions demonstrates its existence. Moreover, it is not surprising that the depth and damage of the American individualism are difficult to recognize. For many years, believing that French individualism was the worst (at least French were Number One in something!), I underestimated the roots and destructive power of North American individualism. We do not pay much attention to the air we breathe at each inhalation. We start looking at the composition of the air when it becomes too polluted or rarefied. Similarly, individualism is what everyone breathes from morning to evening in this country. It is prevalent in many aspects of our lives. Without it people are afraid they might suffocate. They are apprehensive of any restrictive structure, labeling it authoritarian. They feel that limitations imposed by any group life are oppressive.

To fear suffocation is an important and healthy reaction. The Canadian philosopher Charles Taylor made a sharp analysis of the ethics of authenticity[62] which has ties with that aspect of individualism under discussion here. Authenticity is "the finest achievement of modern civilization." He says, "We live in a world where people have a right to choose for themselves their own pattern of life, to decide in conscience what convictions to espouse, to determine the shape of their lives in a whole host of ways that their ancestors couldn't control."[63] Taylor points out that the wish for self-realization so prevalent today, crumbling the social commitment and other traditional values, accompanies the search for an authentic and true self which should be separated from various superficial false selves—often imposed by social expectations and patterns. "They develop their own form of life, grounded on their own sense of what is really important or of value." People feel that they ought to pursue self realization[64] to be true to themselves.

This ethic of authenticity might be the most important treasure of the North American culture. It is expressed often by the words freedom, liberty or autonomy, but it is the call for authenticity arising inside the human, which is at the origin and which gives a firm foundation to this fascinating aspect of the American culture. On the other hand, this richness carries in itself the danger of a self-centeredness, bringing very destructive consequences. There is no reason to be surprised by this ambivalence. These two aspects of the authenticity quest arise from the paradox of the human condition. Everyone is called to discover one's true-self, conscious that nobody can replace him/her in that journey and unable to realize that discovery by oneself alone.

The requirement for authenticity, result of an inner revolt, produces fruits of truth and freedom. This quest for authenticity did not grow alone, and the unhealed wounds received by the forefathers brought simultaneously an important component to the culture: a wounded anthropology. The widely accepted vision of the person, exemplified in the self-made man model, causes extremely destructive violence. It might even be **the most destructive of the causes specific to the North American culture,** as its repercussions appear in almost every area of personal and social life.

The traditional gospel-fed anthropology states that the person cannot come to reality without various sets of relationships that we described before. These authentic relationships with our own shadow, with others, with God, and with the created world foster the recognition of the sacred inside all creatures, friend and foe alike. This challenges the person in formation. A truncated understanding of the person impedes the experience of some of these sacred ties and undervalues most of them. As a consequence, the acknowledgment and influence of the sacred regresses in the cultural North American field of influence. The self-made man brings more damages than it was thought when he was admired on his pedestal.

When people do not strive for wholeness, their distorted vision of the human being favors the growing market world. A large majority of people attempts to fill the void of their incompleteness with objects offered by the consumption society. "I shop therefore I am" says a bumper sticker. This correlation between inner emptiness and consumption has often been pointed out.[65] It is a drama to witness how eagerly one attempts to fill an inner void with "stuff." The weeds of greed, the Number One syndrome, and the self-made man model compete to occupy the empty space inside the human being. Marketing agents know that their success is more certain when they address people separately, considered as individuals and not as persons involved in relationships. "You can decide yourself," they say to the children, "you are old enough." "If you want it, you buy it," they tell the teens. "You do not need to ask your partner, the down payment is only a few dollars." These are common slogans. Market society's organizational dynamic is powerful and its damages to the sacredness, the pearl inside any being, are profound. Deeply frustrated human beings often violently express their willingness to survive this contempt of their preciousness.

People who have been raised with erroneous notions and whose culture gives credit to these faulty principles will not change easily. Only the painful experience of failures may bring new life as it shakes the bases of one's existence and forces reevaluation. The first requirement is recognition of one's own incompleteness and to touch it deeply. This experience might seem traumatic at first! To survive the experience of a void, and realize that an important part of oneself is missing, opens the door to a better teaching on the human person and for the richness of the Gospel vision. This fills their inner longing. Is there a greater experience than personal fulfillment through a nurturing relationship? It is the most common way to experience entry into one's full being. The ethic of authenticity recognizes the value of this experience and search for truth.

It is encouraging that the latter part of the twentieth century witnessed efforts to help people nurture interpersonal relationships. Counselors, group therapists and psychologists are everywhere in the U.S. Unfortunately, many patterns of our culture are weighing in the opposite direction and decrease the efficiency of these interesting efforts. During the last few decades many who long for community as a luxury or a security now realize that they cannot become a complete person unless they accept the exigencies of community relationships. In the U.S. there is a renewal of various communities: neighborhoods, common interest communities, faith communities, therapeutic gatherings and even attempts to build a democracy concerned about local matters whose size is not overwhelming. These new realizations are promising and should be commended. Participating in community life might be an easier way to concretely recognize the nurturing role of relationships and the longing to become fully human. While no group is perfect, to walk alone in an effort to reform society [66] damages deeply those who do so. Whatever the constructive expressions of the American individualism, such as the quest for authenticity, the role model of the self-made man—the lone ranger—brings violence to the individual and to society.

Questions for Reflection

- *What do you feel is the most important in the last chapter?*

- *What does this chapter stir in you?*

- *Search examples of violences coming from the vision that the person to grow needs only courage and that relationships are a luxury?*

- *Do you consider it an exaggeration to say that the anthropology which sustains the self-made man, is the most destructive element of the American culture? Why or why not?*

- *How can we remedy the damages of such distorted anthropology?*

- *Do you feel that you can be called an individualist person? What are your thoughts about the four types of relationships mentioned in this chapter?*

- *Have you experienced how being an active member of a community or a group gave you a feeling of wholeness and allowed you to discover in yourself qualities and inner richness that you did not know?*

- *Can you cite a few examples of self-service where you can name some important disadvantages? Even violences against groups or communities?*

CHAPTER SEVEN

Facing the Tangled Roots
of Violence

Many Dynamisms Involved in Violence

L ED BY THE HYPOTHESIS that seldom-discussed assumptions within the principles of the U.S. culture foster various violences, our reflection in the last four chapters focused on the main causes of violence flowing out of the principles of the American Way of Life itself. Did I credit wrongly the American Way of Life for being at the origin of some violences that, some people maintain, may find their roots in the whole of Western culture?

Everyone can give examples of the emerging presence of *market values* in the Western world at large. Does it come from the cultural values common to Western Europe and countries populated by Western Europe emigration? Or is it coming principally from the influence of the values recognized inside the United States and conveyed outside the country? Various initiatives of the U.S. policy for spreading values recognized inside U.S. business circles offer a frightening list. This leads me to credit the U.S. culture for the presence, in other parts of the world, of the destructive values that I pointed out.

In 1944 before the end of the War, the Bretton Woods Conference[67] gave to the U.S. dollar the status of the international change currency, replacing the British pound. The U.S.A. committed themselves to exchange dollars for gold whenever it would be required. This part of the Agreement and the important participation of the U.S.A. in the World Bank [68], and the International Monetary Fund (IFM) gave a leading role to the U.S.A.[69] The decisions of the Federal Reserve had repercussions the world over. The values embedded in the U.S. culture spread subtly or were imposed by the old market praxis that the most important lender can make the law in any deal. In international official bodies, decisions were taken by the U.S. government, but these were in tune with the values of the U.S. culture. One sign of that accord was the absence of any strong protest inside the nation, as it has been frequent with other violations of traditional values of the U.S. culture. Many North Americans are still unaware that their government had unilaterally denounced the convertibility dollar-gold to which the U.S. committed themselves. Shockingly, the wealth of the country prevailed without question over a solemn signature. The same prevalence of material interests over any moral considerations appeared in the various "rounds" of the General Agreement on Tariffs and Trade (G.A.T.T.) and the attempt to establish the Multilateral Agreement on Investments (M.A.I.).[70] In other developed and developing countries the undemocratic secret preparation of the M.A.I. provoked reactions. In the U.S.A. a friend of mine who owns a bank was even ignorant of the M.A.I. project. One year after international protests started, mention of the M.A.I. appeared in the alternative U.S. media. With the convulsions of the financial markets and the plunge of the Dow in September 1998, *Time* magazine and *Newsweek* quoted experts wondering if an uncontrolled market is really suitable. The leading role of the U.S in the preparation of the G.A.T.T. and the M.A.I. was nurtured by the true allergy of North American people to any control by political or administrative authorities. The reality is that the financial powers, de facto control the economic situation and present their control as a Law of the Universe.

In *Newsweek*, Robert J. Samuelson wrote: "Market capitalism is not just an economic system. It is also a set of cultural values that emphasizes the virtue of competition, the legitimacy of profit and the value of freedom."[71] The U.S.A. has been and is the major advocate of 'market capitalism' and its dynamism. The world over, the global culture where a market culture assumes that it has the right to establish the principles of morality, seems really to be an export of the U.S.A. The fact that other countries and cultures imitate or support the U.S. initiatives does not diminish the role of the U.S.

I credited the *colonial past* of the U.S.A. for a set of violences: one of these is a racist policy that had violated so many treaties solemnly signed by the Congress with the Indian Nations. This racist policy continues to disdain the rights of various Tribes and Nations. Certainly, most of the Western countries have racist behaviors and sometimes racist policies, but none had conquered its own territory over natives and has had slaves for more than three centuries.[72]

More than this direct oppression of the Native Americans, I related the oppression brought by the American Way of Life upon people of other countries, to the time when North Americans were themselves oppressed by their mother-country. This is a unique situation in the Western World.

People may be inclined to compare the North American messianism and its Number One complex to the French and the Spanish arrogance arising from a similar complex and sense of mission. Nevertheless, I see important differences, mainly that France and Spain referred to a mission that they asked the Church to give to them, whereas the colonizers of North America understood their sacred mission as coming directly from God himself. The certitude of a Manifest Destiny of the American people, that continues to give foundation or to cover new forms of imperialism, does not seem to have an equivalent in any other part of the world.

I gave major credit to *the self-made* man mentality and the anthropology that allowed his birth for being the root of specific violence and for helping the growth of the market place. It favored the substitution of the values of human centered culture by values of the market praxis. The self-made man is truly an American creation. The anthropology that I see having consequences on violence had been credited by Max Weber for the growth of capitalism. **My point is that the specific type of American individualism exemplified by the self-made man gave to the substitution of market values for human centered values, a dynamism simultaneously subtle and extremely powerful.**

These are the main reasons why I credit the U.S. culture and not other cultures for the roots I discussed. The emerging "global culture" is for a large part the result of the spreading of U.S. values. If people want to credit this new reality for the violences I listed, they will have to recognize the determining action of the U.S. culture in the arising of new global values.

I have intentionally not considered the violences taking roots in realities other than the particular U.S. culture. Ethicists, sociologists, and politicians have written well documented reflections on the gender violence common to western and most eastern cultures and on violences coming from one culture imposed upon another. Anthropologists, psychologists, and philosophers have studied violences which have their origin in the nature of the human being and its most common reactions, such as fear, anger, the mimetic rivalry deeply rooted inside human nature, and scapegoating with its religious motivations. Adding to these studies of the human condition, more scholars have examined the violences coming from the growth of cities at the expense of traditional social ties. Western civilization is, without doubt, the deeper cause of the global urban mushrooming. This growth uproots people from land and villages and throws them into a man-made environment and cramped space in the heart of the cities, all of which are credited for most of the urban violence. Not included are the violences that arise from occasional political or economic events. They bring drama and suffering, but are outside the limits of this exploration of the U.S. culture through my personal experience. I hope these precisions will help avoiding the possible confusion between these roots of violence and what comes specifically from the American Way of Life.

Even such a limited investigation brings to light an overwhelming list of roots of violence. A culture is not the result of a rational process and less of a democratic choice. This may discourage anyone who tries to understand what is going on inside a way of life. A culture grows under various subtle interactions, and most of the time the leading forces do not give their name. People who want to consciously influence their culture generally cannot identify the forces and links of causes they have to act upon.

The causes of violence explored in the previous chapters grew on various grounds: A truncated anthropology resulting from wounds contracted in the Old Countries and giving an erroneous understanding of human growth; various scars inherited from a colonial past that started as a heroic adventure; desires and passions common in every human being but fueled by the abundance of land and resources; an American dream; an ambiguous special destiny; and a market culture subtly replacing any previous values of the culture. This is not an exhaustive list. These various causes form a compact set where interactions are crisscrossing and mixing at various levels. It is not surprising that they intermingle with other roots of violence not specific to the North American culture, such as greed, the desire to dominate, or the uprooting from the land. **We need to understand some of the dynamisms of these causes and their interactions in order to prioritize our efforts for transformation into a more humane and just situation.**

Some people claim that for any transformation we need to examine all the sources of violence at the same time. They establish a list of violences so extensive that they become lost in a lengthy enumeration of causes and roots. I am of the opinion that we do not need to fight all the manifestations of violence at once as it is impossible to heal all that needs to be remedied. Our responsibilities are more limited. Scholars may dig harder, searching for the ultimate roots of violence, which may be the lack of spiritual development. The pragmatic approach followed in this text comes more from a personal experience, and less from a scholarly, exhaustive investigation and analysis. It wants to help those involved in practical changes so that they can focus their efforts on what they can reach and be more efficient. Our common responsibilities arise from living in a specific culture, in a limited territory, at a unique time. This context of our existence limits our means of action for the transformation of the political and cultural causes of violence.

From Cultural Roots to Violence Itself

By what process do some realities of the culture give birth to violence? According to accepted authorities, **power** and **desire** seem the most common forces acting between the potential violence and the violence itself.

Any direct or indirect attack on dignity brings feelings of frustration and anger to the victims, who express their feelings violently in order to prove their existence and gain at least some consideration. Rollo May in *Power and Innocence*[73] describes this in five levels of **power** present as potentialities in every human being's life: 1) the power to be; 2) self-affirmation; 3) self-assertion; 4) development of aggression when self-assertion is blocked; 5) violence as ultimate explosion if all efforts toward aggression are ineffective. This schematic explanation elucidates why negligence, scorn, refusal and attack against dignity or sacredness are conducive to violence and why the time and the intensity of the violence can vary. If these claims of the person are not recognized, violence explodes either at any level of a frustrated power or as the final and more powerful manifestation of this force. In considering people as commodities, the culture born from the market encircles persons with a pervasive neglect of the richness that every human perceives deep inside, at least in a confused manner. This is the de-humanization we mentioned previously. The inner treasure has been despised, the power tied to the human quality of the person has been frustrated. This subtle violence gives birth to open violence, or to a wound hard to heal.

These frustrations arising from the core of the person suffering from the lack of recognition and power are not the only ones. René Girard and Gil Baillie recall the importance of mimic desire at the source of various violences. Imitation of others is part of the human tendencies. Artificial develop-

ing of *wants* impossible to satisfy brings a multitude of frustrations. This comes from the dominant role of the market place
that offers a huge variety of items and services, and persuades
people they really need them. In every poor neighborhood
where I lived the breaking in of houses increased during
periods of greater advertising, especially Christmas. How can
people resist the desire to have what everyone has and what
the media and displays of merchandise suggestively offer all
the day long? The lack of money needed to fulfill the wishes
creates a sharp pain exploding in violence.

Other frustrations come from models which are also out
of reach. Success models carried by the culture exalted at
school or by the media, or moral models commended by
religions all discourage individuals who, realizing their limits,
feel unable to approach these ideal examples. These models
presented as a standard accomplishment, develop a complex
of culpability in those who fail to reach these heights. Unfulfilled **desire** gives place to frustration which grows, brews
inside the person, or explodes. It was simultaneously comic
and dramatic to hear fellow day laborers, sleeping on the
streets because of instability or alcoholism, commenting that
it was their own fault if they did not accede to high responsibilities. At school they heard that "any citizen of the country
can become President of the U.S.A.," and naively they believed that statement. This too frequent presentation of
moral accomplishment models or of social success weighs
heavily on millions of people frustrated at being short of
breath and energy in their attempt to reach peaks beyond
their potential. There are plenty of discouraged, unsuccessful
self-made men. Often they are bitter or violent. Psychological
or spiritual counselors complain about such oppressive models. In all these cases of frustrations, the mimic desire to
imitate the model, as René Girard describes it, has been

exacerbated and has remained unfulfilled. The wound is wide open and deep. Its violent consequences will not be remedied by more police and more prisons.

A similar psychological process of tension towards a goal and frustration caused by failing, seems at work with the national desire to fulfill the divine mission that most American people believe to have received, and then realize it might be out of reach. Some people may think that God did not give the universal mission to create a perfect community to American people, but to humankind. Others stubbornly attempt to accomplish the demands of Manifest Destiny at any cost, including violence. For others anger grows out of disappointment and this brings more violence.

These dynamics involving power and desire are those which allow the roots of violence to visibly manifest their destructive potentialities. They are like bridges between cultural roots and violence with its so-varied manifestations. Are you not seeing like I do, these psychological dynamics at work? Knowing the exact role of the realities of power and desire should help us avoid the frequent confusion of mistaking them for the roots of violence. At least in the case of the violences specific to the American Way of Life, they are not the cultural roots. These psychological realities common to all humans, intermingle with the cultural roots. Even though cultural principles will need a long time for any transformation, they will change quicker than human nature. Now we will next examine the interactions of the main cultural roots that we identified in the previous chapters.

Greed and Individualism Nurturing Market Culture

The market culture itself would not have developed in the amazing way it did without the greed that dwells in every human. Anxiety about the future and fear of lacking power are most likely the seeds of greed. Only those who receive their security from the relationships of a social fabric and from an alive relationship with the Creator can lower their eagerness for possessions. These free people find their security and joy not in accumulating, not in owning, but in relating. Sometimes they abandon as much as they can of their possessions in order to let relationships grow, as ownership often brings disputes and destroys ties.[74] Some want to be free from any slavery to possession. They experience their participation in an unlimited and fulfilling richness: God's richness and the richness of the sacred recognized in others.

I understand that the search for security and power developed quickly when settlers arrived in a huge territory gifted by abundant land with rich soil and resources seemingly unlimited. During three and half centuries immigrants, even with well-rooted religious faith and moral principles, easily listened to the sirens of greed, making increased wealth their priority. The belief that wealth is part of the Creator's call to a very special manifest destiny at the service of the whole of humankind gave free rein to a natural tendency. Nothing then could impede a market society from launching without restraint a market culture imposing its own set of values. Market culture develops wildly and spreads its violence all over the world since it follows the penetration of businesses built on the principles of economic rationalism that pretend to be inescapable.

Would the market culture have reached its seductive and destructive development without the omnipresent individualism? This one is largely a result of the self-made man's conception of life. I am convinced that the market culture became a cancer inside the North American culture because of the presence inside the American Way of Life of the truncated anthropology described earlier. European and Asian cultures emphasize relationships more. Their communitarian barriers play a regulating function to the developing market. Without these safeguards human tendencies and passions can pursue their course, freely. Greed is nurtured by individualism. The other side of the coin shows humanness and sacredness submerged and tarnished.

Previously I pointed out how the values of the market society have insidiously replaced principles of the culture held in previous generations. Our own behaviors, public opinion, and the reflections of well-listened-to personalities of our time create the belief that the principles of the market culture are unquestionable. Some people present them as the laws of the universe. Others recognize them as waves of the ocean, and accept obeying their power and being carried by them, even if they do not like it. Are market principles like ordinary waves shaking the previous culture or are they like a tidal wave destroying irresistibly? It might be neither one. My sense is that it is more than an ordinary wave. It is a tidal wave, but its destruction is not total. Those who are conscious of what is happening can act to rediscover the sacredness, this profound foundation of our own being, which has been neglected and eroded but is still there as a hard diamond, tiny but sending its sparkles. These persons need to open themselves to recognize that sacredness still resides in the core of other beings. This consciousness is essential in resisting the attacks of the market culture.

The destructiveness of the market culture should not be underestimated. The subtle way by which that new culture despises the sacredness of human beings and all of creation is dramatic in magnitude. In the past that violence was moderate, but now it has become the worst violence done to human beings and all living creatures who have in them the divine mark of their common Creator.

Other Cultural Roots of Violence

We need to examine the interconnectedness of the other cultural roots of violence previously listed: how the violences coming from the colonial origin of the country—racism, oppression of minorities and less developed countries, Messianism and the Number One complex—interact with other roots or dynamisms of violence.

Racism is not a U.S. specialty. Many human groups are afflicted by its destructive action. In the case of the specific U.S. racism towards Native Americans and Afro-Americans, grown inside the unique American history, we can state that greed helped racism to develop. Taking rich lands from the Natives' territory and enslaving Africans in order to export more minerals or more crops reinforced the undiscussed principle of the colonial culture: the primacy of the whites over any colored person. The values of the Anglo culture that gave birth to the market culture caused uneasiness of the minorities and widened the gap between the majority and minorities' cultures. Daily violences continue to victimize the members of minorities.

The American Messianism interacted with racism as people of color were not invested with the same mission. They were supposed to benefit from the moral mission of service to the whole of humankind received by the whites. Native Americans also claimed to have received, from the Creator, the mission to be good stewards of Mother Earth and of all their "relations." This did not receive serious attention until recently from a small minority of whites. Messianism and Manifest Destiny of the American nation helped the search for material prosperity, along with the omnipresent greed that infiltrates such a pursuit. The understanding, deeply present in the U.S. culture, of God as protector of wealth and giving through richness a sign of predestination, strengthened the belief in Messianism and Manifest Destiny with its sequence of violences. The coherence between these various notions impedes even good people from seeing how these ideas about God and God's mission are nurturing violence.

The Number One complex dwelling inside a person, a group or the nation, expresses a competitive mentality that favors domination. Very young children learn competition, then sports competition is taught in school and sometimes developed to an extreme point in college. During adult life the Number One syndrome is easily adopted by fear of losing a preeminent financial status that makes possible the American Way of Life. This is the opposite of a mentality of interdependence, complementarity and solidarity. With such a competitive and dominative mentality, true relationships are almost impossible, as dialogue is not sought. Hidden or open conflicts develop. At the national level the Number One state of mind is often presented as a moral mission sustaining military and economic leaders in a missionary zeal. The rhetoric used during the Gulf War of 1991 by President George Bush and other leaders gave a dramatic example of the intermixing of the Number One complex, the divine mission of the nation, and greed connected with the imperatives of market culture. This frequently irritates foreigners aware of this ridiculous pretentiousness as a source of dramatic violence. Asian and Middle East countries, heirs of millennia-old cultures, frequently manifested their exasperation during recent decades, to the surprise of many Americans.

These are the main data of the U.S. culture that intermix, strengthening each other and making the American Way of Life so conducive to violence. However painful it is to face this reality, it is essential to look at it. When our loved ones are sick, the denial of their illness is no gain either for them or for us. In previous pages I invited the readers to reflect with me on a few of my experiences and to do similar reflection on their own experiences. This requires us to look without defensiveness at the principles on which our Way of Life is built — seeing both the flaws and the beneficial effects. I brought my little participation to the diagnosis of the illness of the cultural violence, even though I knew the pain or anger that some people will feel in reading these few pages. Truth makes us free. Otherwise freedom does not exist.

Questions for Reflection

* *In your own life, what causes of violence can you identify?*

* *How does your own cultural background foster violence?*

* *From your experience what would you add or suppress in the description of the various factors of violence mentioned in the previous chapter?*

* *How does greed affect you? your friends?*

* *How important are the relationships in your life?*

* *Do you know examples of principles of the market culture that became prevalent in using a rationale based on the truncated anthropology shown in the self-made man?*

Afterword

Towards Healing by a Nonviolent Culture

L IKE THE HEALING OF A PERSON, the healing of a nation or of a culture requires a good diagnosis before the choice of a medicine. Too many discourses on the North American violence offer remedies without the analysis leading to a well-established diagnosis. Some discourses aiming at a diagnosis do not look further than the immediate causes of violence. They often have no idea that the principles of the culture can be incriminated. This short-sighted method has brought disappointing solutions. Good-hearted people continue to recommend new laws, more police, more prisons, or a rekindling of moralism. None of these can heal the principles on which our culture is established. Some roots of our Way of Life developed during the colonial era, others during the national history after Independence and some more recently, coming from the changes inside the market world.

In the previous chapters it became clearer that some areas of our behavior will demand a gigantic effort of transformation. Only a persevering intellectual, moral and structural effort can change the wide-spread mentality concerning the becoming of a person. To clearly establish limits on market laws so that they do not continue to twist our culture, will demand lucidity, cleverness and fortitude.

This impressive and long-term effort can receive help from the recent growing consciousness of environmental problems. The violence done to the earth, capable of jeopardizing the future of the planet, has opened many eyes to the subtle violence done to humanness. If the ecological movement understands better that the future of the planet depends on a nonviolent way of life, a well founded hope can develop and bear fruit.

Material measures, however sophisticated, cannot succeed in healing the American culture. Anthropological and spiritual vision requires a deep transformation of people. A moral reform alone, without ties to a methodology for transformation of the structures, will be without grasp on a culture invaded by the market principles and its reduction of every reality into profit figures. Facing the difficulty of discovering a process having both spiritual and structural effects, some people, aware of the dimensions of the crisis, are discouraged.

I have reflected too on the best means to bring some healing to a culture pregnant with incredible possibilities, but which is involved in a world-wide process of destruction of humanness and sacredness. I followed with interest the reflections and actions of Vaclav Havel from Czechoslovakia and of Vitaltas Lansbirgis from Lithuania who trusted nonviolence for freeing their countries dominated by the Stalinist culture. For decades, nonviolence has been considered only as an interesting way of conflict resolution, even as a powerful method for social change, or as a possible pathway for an oppressed group or nation to obtain its independence. Only feeble voices pointed out the possibilities of nonviolence for a "total revolution"[75] which does not mean only a turnover of power holders, but a complete change of mentality and structures.

The last hundred years have allowed us to witness many examples of decreasing violence through using the spirit and the method systematized by the Mahatma Gandhi. The last two decades witnessed amazing successes of nonviolence in various continents. Studies are available everywhere in a growing number of languages showing nonviolent resolution of conflicts in a wide array of situations. The spirit and the methodology of nonviolence are at the disposition of whomever wants to have the courage to put them into practice. Monographs of actions, interviews of direct actors and various involvements in nonviolent actions sustained my reflections, and my confidence in the nonviolent process. I was delighted when on November 20, 1997, the General Assembly of the UN accepted a proposal of the UNESCO to make the year 2000 a year for a peace culture, and found more encouragement when twenty Nobel Peace Prize Laureates asked the United Nations to start the millennium with a *decade of nonviolence* for building a nonviolent *culture*. This last project accepted in November 1998 is the sign that nonviolence is being looked at by people from the grass roots level to the decision-makers for national and international policies. Facing injustices or violences, more people are searching for a true remedy, not just a band-aid. They reject the method of using fire against the fire, destroying everything in its way.

Eradicating the true roots of the violence is the only hope for healing the violence dwelling inside a culture. My confidence in a nonviolent culture for healing the North American violent culture has grown slowly but is strengthening every day. The principles of this way of life go to the center of problems; however, their power has not yet been explored on a large scale at the level of a culture. How can this change take place? What are the aspects of the nonviolent spirit and process that can have the most important role in this change?

Nonviolence builds its strength on the importance of **relationships**. It refuses the division between good people and bad people—the multi-centenary manicheism. It is based on the reality of the presence of good and of bad co-existing inside every single person. Nonviolent strategy calls those who are now faithful to the good present inside them, to awaken the good inside their adversaries who at that same moment serve violence or injustice. This dynamic is built on confidence in the divine power of the good and its unity. Nonviolent strategy for conflict resolution aims at promoting a new stage in which the good of my adversary and the good that is in me both collaborate to find a more just solution. The generally accepted dynamics is that one side needs to win and the other lose. Both camps should be winners, avoiding the bitterness of a defeated one who continues the cycle of violence by preparing revenge as soon as possible. This commonly used spiral of violence[76] can only aggravate and widen the conflict. In an alternative way, M.K. Gandhi and Nelson Mandella struggling for the independence of their people, gave us remarkable examples of their eagerness to continue to respect their opponents and collaborate with them. Looking back at the independence of India, at the Civil Rights Movement of Martin Luther King Jr., at the downfall of the communist regime in U.S.S.R., or at the end of the apartheid in South Africa, we are encouraged. Nonviolent struggle avoided foreseen blood baths and opened the way for a constructive future.

Nonviolence is never satisfied only by the absence of violence. It is a spirit and a methodology aimed at disarming an opponent and destroying the germs of violence. Present and future sources of conflicts are targets of a peaceful and respectful disarming. The nonviolent method includes the refusal to use any tricks. It avoids words and actions which might incite the actor of injustice to become more aggressive.

How can this method apply to the violence caused by the market culture? The market culture impedes sacredness from revealing its presence and obtaining recognition. It discards the value of sacredness in the name of effectiveness. **Nonviolence resists this stance, and proclaims that the freeing and growing of sacredness is an important element for a real efficiency.** Nonviolence has shown its amazing results in saving human lives by the millions and in avoiding considerable material destruction. Moreover, nonviolence destroys the germs of violence by recognizing the dignity of humanness inside the antagonists. Nonviolent strategy is attentive to the liberation of the captive sacredness in whoever is violent or unjust. These are the main reasons why the nonviolent resolution of conflicts is so appropriate for the change from a culture of violence to a culture of relationships.

In a culture of relationships the importance of various nurturing communities is central. It is one of the reasons why Mahatma Gandhi promoted ashrams (communities) of satyagrahis, for the nonviolent volunteers. For any healing of the North American culture, a tremendous effort will be needed to find new ways of building challenging communities. Probably one of the most promising realizations of nonviolence in the U.S.-Anglo milieu is the creation, over the last 20 years, of *affinity groups*. Established at first for practical and tactical reasons in order to prepare for a nonviolent action, they became in many places nurturing communities. Nonviolent struggle, especially when directed at cultural principles of a nation, cannot be only the sum of individual efforts. It will require an impressive mobilization of energies to build the needed network of communities. This might be the most challenging aspect of the nonviolent proposal to change the culture, to heal the individualism of the self-made model. Will there be enough willingness to accept the various requirements of groups and communities? In my desire to be honest with the readers, I have to admit this is where I am not completely sure such a willingness will be stirred up before it is too late!

An aspect of a culture of relationships is the structure of the various groups and societies. The pyramidal model so frequent in the dominant culture in the U.S.A. will need to be replaced by the circular model used in consensus groups and in the Native American tribes. This will require creativity, as the technical complexity of many matters tends towards centralization, where a few people have the last say in the centers of decision, be they financial, military or even informational. This is shown in a graphic manner by the nuclear suitcase accompanying the Presidents of Russia and of the U.S.A. in all their travels, allowing them to start a nuclear war without a congressional vote. Nonviolent culture, which needs charismatic animating figures, will have to deal with such important problems of the pyramidal structure. Some people think that a solution might come with the e-mail. That is not yet obvious.

Since greed amplifies some of the roots of violence specific to the U.S, nonviolence which trusts inner strength in opposing a material violent strength, does not seek to accumulate wealth and all that it procures. Material power is too ambiguous and less worthy of trust than the inner source of power. Greed has very little grip on individuals, groups, and small societies established on nonviolence.

Those who trust in nonviolence for any change are not blind to the limits in the willingness of their adversary to change. The conversion of the opponent touched by the disarming behavior of the nonviolent person willing to suffer if needed, is an ideal difficult to reach. In a nonviolent struggle, strategy attempts to provoke a change inside the adversary through the power of truth and love. If such a change does not occur, then strategy strives with a more powerful mass movement to exert constraint so that the opponent feels compelled in *his own interest* to accept the just demands of his adversary. In both processes of the non violent actions, respect for the sacredness of the adversary is a fundamental element.

In Gandhi's campaign non-cooperation is the first step for a social group in expressing its dignity and its willingness to suffer in order to obtain change. The many destructive aspects of the market culture and of the conception of the human being which are strengthening this damaging culture, challenge nonviolent strategists to invent new ways of enfleshing non-cooperation. For now, the boycott seems the most appropriate means to express non-cooperation with the market culture, as it hits the opponent's wallet by reducing profit. When the motivation of boycott is the dignity of the human being who is not for sale, it exerts a powerful attraction to that nonviolent technique. The boycotts led by the longshoremen during the Vietnam war and the war in El Salvador, the boycott of the Montgomery buses, those led by César Chavez with the United Farm Workers, and by the group INFACT[77] have acquired a glow and a mobilizing effect on a large part of public opinion. These are encouraging examples for building a strategy efficient for the long term.

Non-cooperation calls for the move towards an alternative. Some nonviolent groups do not understand that refusing one's assent is not sufficient. It may give a "good conscience" to a few, but might not bring the expected changes. Dissent through actions of non-cooperation should lead to the creation of alternative structures, shaping the future and involving the participation of huge numbers of people. This is part of the nonviolent process. It may start with a few persons, but it should involve huge crowds, not only because their pressure on the violent will be greater, but because those involved become transformed by their commitment to obtain a desired end. Moreover, it gives to the future of the nonviolent culture a wider and more promising base.

M.K. Gandhi, launching the boycott of the "made in England" cottonades, encouraged Indians to spin and weave their home grown cotton. The Albanian majority in Kosova,[78] forbidden to receive teaching in their language, created alternative underground schools and even a university. In the U.S.A., cooperatives of sellers or buyers, credit unions, and land trusts are at the forefront of the alternative field. Moreover, on the international level some groups give microloans for creating new structures. Others like *Pueblo to People,* or *Equal Exchange,* which develop direct sale from Third World agricultural or crafts cooperatives to American buyers, play an important educative role.[79] Unfortunately, some agricultural cooperatives and some credit unions, when growing, enter into the corporate model and follow the market laws. It requires perseverance to maintain alternative structures based on relationships and solidarity and not on economic rationalism. It requires shaking off passivity and motivating people to accept a personal sacrifice. The cooperative structures, whatever their legal status, have an irreplaceable role in showing concrete ways of keeping the human person at the center of a Way of Life.

In his recent book, *The Sibling Society*, Robert Bly follows some others who state that the people growing up in the North American culture either have been deeply damaged during the first years of life, losing adaptability, or are unwilling to develop creativity and adaptability. This situation would be the cause of the passivity to which the TV has subjected people. Robert Bly points out another difficulty in becoming a person active in one's own life and participating in the life of the world: the trauma suffered during the first years of childhood by a surrounding which favored passivity.[80] I lean towards these explanations.[81] Many authors have observed too that the survival of democracy and of the human race need an active participation of at least a large minority. These people work to help large numbers become more human by their participation in the common adventure of humanity. This is an important challenge for the new millenary. New teaching methods developed during the last half-century, and the brilliant input brought by Paolo Freiere, will most likely be the foundations for any progress into increasing the active participation of more citizens.

Nonviolence is not an easy way. It requires people not afraid to challenge their own mentality, the behaviors of others, and the structures of society. I am not elaborating on a detailed nonviolent proposal for healing the principles of the American Way of Life. Three reasons direct my choice: it will need a rigorous analysis, it could be the topic of a book in itself, and it will require a wider perception of the attack on humanness. That consciousness is a prerequisite for any motivation. Any strategy needs to evaluate the dynamism of motivated people able to be agents of change.

Some Principles of a Nonviolent Culture

Even though it is not possible to describe now the phases of transformation of the American culture we can tentatively list some principles of a nonviolent culture:

1. **The human beings do not exist without relationships.** It is through a set of relationships that an individual having a human body starts to exist and becomes a person.

2. **The human dignity should not be alienated.** Everyone has to claim one's own dignity and recognize the dignity of others. This means those who are accomplices of evil by their passivity when submitted to violence and injustice are called to rise against the destruction of their own sacredness: it is a treasure of the human race. On the other hand, the evildoers should have their dignity or humanness respected as an absolute, whatever evil they perpetrate.

3. **All of creation, animate or inanimate, is sacred,** and should be respected by humans. A spirit of domination and exploitation does not revere that sacredness.

4. **Means that do not respect the human dignity and other expressions of the good cannot be used even for beneficial results.** "The means may be likened to a seed, the end to a tree, and there is just the same inviolable connection between the means and the end as there is between the seed and the tree."[82] The end is worth what the means are worth.

5. **The same good with its power exists inside each of the opponents** during a conflict. Each one has inside oneself the good and the bad, as evil finds complicity in everyone. When love and truth are inactive or enslaved inside evildo-

ers, the respect they receive for their sacredness, dignity or humanness can awaken them to their inner value.

6. **The power of truth and love, that has a divine origin, is greater than any other power** (brute force; psychological power; wealth). It changes both opponents entangled in conflicts.

Relationships recognizing the dignity of the opponents can disarm their hostile behaviors

7. **The collective expression of the inner power requires a certain level of social cohesion.** Transformation of a damaging culture needs the constraint of a great number of united people. The collective struggle for common values strengthens the social cohesion.

8. **The challenge of communities and the pursuit of the common good are a requisite** for building the nonviolent culture that is done by and for the masses. It is not an elitist culture.

9. **Nobody has the whole truth. No culture has the whole truth. Each one sees and serves only a part of the truth.** For a better apprehension of the truth, relationships between people and cultures should abandon a vertical pattern for a circular one of people seeing the diverse aspects of truth. This makes relationships truer to the complexity of reality.

10. **To accept the risk to suffer rather than to impose suffering on others** is a frequent requirement of love inside the nonviolent culture. In that culture of relationships, the positive aspect of self-accepted suffering reveals what values are cherished.

All Spiritual People of the Country,. Unite!

In seeking to bring some clarity to the roots of violence and the principles of a nonviolent culture, I hope to participate in motivating people. Perhaps in this writing many flaws of the U.S. culture have become more evident and frightening. **The market culture is suffocating the center of our being.** The special individualism of the self-made man that is one of the causes of this culture collaborates in the human suffocation. Racism, the Number One complex, the understanding that God is guaranteeing the wealth and has called this nation to a special destiny—all these are roots of additional violence and nurture the power of the market culture. They need to receive the healing that the nonviolent spirit and method offer. A strategy fully adapted to a change needs to be motivated by the inner power of the spirit, otherwise it will be short-lived.

However grim this exploration of the violence dwelling at the core of the American culture appears to be, I am still amazed by the immense potentialities of the North American people. Americans have shown in the past what they were able to do, struggling side by side for change. The struggle against slavery, the unions' dynamism at the end of the 19th century, the Civil Rights movement, and suffragettes' campaign are some of the epic actions of American history. Will we see a beneficial insurrection rooted in the conscience of human beings who refuse to be deprived of their inner richness? This will require that all the spiritual forces of the country unite in that insurrection. The slogan of the Marxist revolution, "Workers of the world, unite!" should be replaced by a call to all people believing in the spiritual core of the humans, **"All spiritual people of the country, unite!"** Will we see people accepting a style of life less lavish so that they

do not become co-opted accomplices of a murderous process? It will require fortitude. Temporary discomfort may
follow. What is at stake is important enough to start changing. Will humanness succeed in placing boundaries on the
market society? Will the human survive in the U.S. culture?

Questions for Reflection

- *Do you feel that the drifting of the U.S. Way of Life towards
  more open or hidden violence is without remedy?*

- *For healing the various ills pointed out in the previous pages:
  Market culture—Racism—Messianism and Manifest Destiny—Number One mentality—Self-made man model and the
  truncated vision of the human person growing, do you see means
  other than nonviolence?*

- *Of all the nonviolent means, what type of action would you
  favor?*

- *Have you participated in previous actions or campaigns of non
  cooperation? What were your motivations? What did it change
  inside you? and in the society?*

- *Have you participated in boycotts? How do you rate the inconvenience for you, your family or your organization in participating in this boycott? Very inconvenient? Not too inconvenient?
  Without effects on you?*

- *Do you know persons who work at building alternatives based
  on relationships?*

Footnotes

Introduction

1. Following the unfortunate common usage, I will often apply the expression "North American" or "American" to a reality specific to the U.S.A., apologizing to Canadians and Mexicans who lament that expression. Their neighbor is not the whole of North America. Other Latin Americans resent the use of the word "Americans" for the exclusive use of people of the U.S.A.

2. Alexis de Tocqueville, *Democracy in America*, Anchor Books.

3. René Girard, *Things Hidden Since the Foundation of the World.* Stanford University Press, 1987.
   René Girard, *Violence and the Sacred.* John Hopkins University Press, 1979.
   Gil Bailie, *Violence Unveiled: Humanity at the Crossroads*, Crossroads, 1995.

4. Two former members of Peace Brigades International, Liam Mahony and Luis Enrique Eguren wrote *Unarmed Bodyguards: Accompaniment for the Protection of Human Rights*, Kumarian Press, 1997. It is a well balanced study of the value and the limits of accompaniment.

Chapter One: What Do We Mean by Violence, Nonviolence, Culture, Market Culture, and Principles?

5. Some people might be surprised by the plural used: injustices and violences. The common use is the singular. Nevertheless at the Pace e Bene Center we think the use of the plural removes the abstract face of the singular. In the tissue of life, violence does not exist, but violences are real, and many!

6. "Satyagraha is as far from passive resistance as the North Pole is from the South" (Gandhi- *Report of the Indian Congress*, 1920, ch. 4).

7. Text taken from *Stride Toward Freedom*, by Martin Luther King, Jr. Harper and Row; pp. 102-107, and shortened by Peter Ediger for Nevada Desert Experience.

8. Raymond Williams, article 'Culture', in *Encyclopedia of Philosophy*, Collier-Mac Millan

9. For a few years I used that expression during workshops and presentations. When I searched this expression in the library, I was amazed not to find it. Doug Glynn in *The Broken Covenant*, Pendle Hill Publications, 1995, uses it occasionally 1 or 2 times (p. 343). Martin J. Wiener, uses it in the title Market Culture, Reckless Passion and 'the Victorian Reconstruction of Punishment' in *The Culture of the Market: Historical essays*, edited by Thomas L. Haskell, Richard P. Teichgraber, Cambridge (G.B) and Cambridge University Press, 1993. The topic itself has been described by other words: consumer culture, commodity form, etc. I prefer the expression 'market culture' which seems to have a wider meaning and be more appropriate.

10. Adam Smith (1723-1790) was influenced by the enthusiasm of his time for Newton and his *The Mathematical Principles of Natural Philosophy (1687)*. "It appears that Adam Smith effectively brought together his socially acceptable understanding of self-interest with his later view of the 'invisible hand' operating in economics analogously to the way gravity operates in physics" (Robert G. Simons, "Is the Gospel Good News for Homo Economicus?" in *The Australasian Catholic Record*, 1995, p. 282, and Robert G. Simons, *Competing Gospels*, E.J. Dwyer, 1995, p. 31)

Chapter Two: Why Were So Many Wonderful Possibilities Not Realized?

11. For example, in place of having newspapers with fewer pages, more than 100 factories were built in 3 years for paper recycling.

12. Harvard professor Robert D. Putnam, communication at the American Political Science Association, September 1995, cf. review in *Commonweal*, Oct. 20, 1995, p. 7. Dr. Putnam in an interview with *Washington Post*, September 3, 1995, said: "The social fabric is becoming visibly thinner, our connections among each other are becoming visibly thinner. We don't trust one another as much, and we don't know one another as much." See also R.D. Putnam, "Bowling Alone: America's Declining Social Capital" in *Journal of Democracy*, Jan. 1995, p. 65 ss. and "Turning in, Turning out: The Strange Disappearance of Social Capital in America" in *Political Science and Politics*, Vol. xxvii- #4, Dec. 1995, pp. 664-683: this last article gives more technical details on his study, and a bibliography.

13. Dr. Rosalie Bertell in *No Immediate Danger*, Women's Press, Toronto, 1985, p. 105 sq. writes: "The global victims of the radiation pollution related to nuclear weapons production, testing, use and waste conservatively number 13 million." She gives detailed estimate figures for various categories of damages.

14. In December 1996, General Andrew Goodpastor, former Allied Commander in Europe joined General Lee Butler, calling for a reduction of the world's nuclear arsenals to very low levels, with the aim of "complete elimination" in the near future. They denounced the "persistent terror filled anesthesia about nuclear arms." Simultaneously 60 generals and admirals, including 17 from the former Soviet Union, echoed these declarations. Invited February 2, 1998, by the National Press Association, General Lee Butler gave more details on his past choices and responsibilities at the Strategic Air Command, and on the reasons for his anti-nuclear stance. He announced that 147 personalities including present and former Chiefs of State or Prime Ministers signed an appeal for complete elimination of nuclear weapons.

15. The subcritical tests do not have a significant nuclear yield. Some people consider them to be a violation of the Comprehensive Test Ban Treaty signed in September 1996. They will provide information for new nuclear weapons, which is contrary to the CTBT and other treaties.

16. President Clinton in his letter to the Senate sent with the CTBT for ratification, describes the policy implemented by his government through the Science-Based Stockpile Stewardship Program (SBSS). It is worth noting his expression "continued progress."

17. Robert Jay Lipton and Richard Falk, in *Indefensible Weapons: The Political and Psychological Case against Nuclearism*, Basic Books, 1982, wrote: "I think it is important to understand that the antidemocratic manner in which nuclear weapons policy has developed over the years makes it confusing for the general public to grasp the central issue, namely the continuous resolve of the U.S. government to defend national interests by relying, as necessary, on nuclear threats" (p. 185)

18. The nuclear clock, officially "the Doomsday clock", is an imaged way to show the threat of a worldwide nuclear catastrophe. Invented by the Bulletin of the Atomic Scientists, its hand is moved by the Board of the Bulletin. In previous years it was set at 2 minutes before midnight, in 1997 it is said to be at 14 minutes to midnight. The nuclear tests in India and Pakistan will surely move back this clock, symbol of the nuclear peril facing humankind.

Chapter Three: Market Culture: Its Emergence and Effects
The topic of this chapter has been explored in the booklet by Alain Richard and Peter Ediger, *Market Culture and Sacredness: Reflections on Violence and Nonviolence in a Market Dominated World,* (Pace e Bene, Occasional Paper Series, No. 3)

19. The organization founded by "Friends of the Earth", produced a videotape "Affluenza" (Bulfrog Films). They described the symptoms of the epidemic : "shopping fever, a rash of debt, overwork, chronic stress, fractured families and resources exhaustion caused by never-ending pursuit of the 'American Dream.'"

20. Paul Wachtel, *The Poverty of Affluence,* New Society Publishers, 1989, is one of the best.

21. In November 1991, the article 27 of the Mexican Constitution of 1917, was revised in order to prepare the way for the signing of N.A.F.T.A. Land reform was terminated, ending any land distribution, and the land belonging to the ejidos and agrarian communities previously untransferable, could then be sold.

22. Interview with subcommandante Marcos, published in *L'Unita* January 4, 1994, English translation in *Voice of Fire,* edited by Ben Clarke and Clifton Ross, New Earth Publications, Berkeley, 1994, p. 47

23. It is not surprising that the three persons who conceived the idea of European Community were humanist Christians: Robert Schuman (France), Konrad Adenauer (Germany), and Alcid De Gaspari (Italy).

24. In Europe the free circulation of persons inside the Community began with tourists, but became applicable progressively to persons with equivalence of diplomas, and then to others.

25. The results of the first two years contradict these hopes. Partly because of the devaluation of the peso, the minimum wage in Mexican factories which was about $5 in 1993 fell to about $2.20 (*The Nation* 1-1-96)

26. See chapter 6, the influence of the model of the self-made facilitated the change of system of reference in the U.S. culture.

27. Even recent authors seem to consider that this opposition resides in the language. cf. Bary Schwartz. *The Battle for Human Nature: Science, Morality and Modern Life,* W.W. Norton, 1986, p. 18

28. John F. Kavanaugh in *Following Christ in a Consumer Society,* Orbis Press, 1981 and second revised edition 1991, uses the expression **Commodity Form of Life** in speaking of a large part of what I call the **Market Culture.** He develops brilliantly how commodification empties the human being of interior reality. It seems that the Market Culture is wider than the Commodity Form of Life, but the analysis

and reflections of John Kavanaugh are a basic reading for anyone who wants to understand the present crisis of values.

29. In July 1944, 44 countries participated in a United Nations Monetary and Financial Conference in Bretton Woods, N.H. This Conference established the bases of the post W.W.II financial functioning, including the International Monetary Fund (IFM) and the International Bank for Reconstruction and Development (IBRD), generally known as World Bank.

30. It should be noted that lately World Bank officials accepted a dialogue with a group of Non Governmental Organizations which were critical of the World Bank policy.

31. The group **Common Cause Corporate Welfare Project** from data available in 1997, estimates the total of "corporate welfare" for the five following years, will be 338 Billions of dollars!

32. In June 1998, the campaign for saving this housing passed a City ballot measure in favor of it. At the time of this writing it is unclear if the right of homeless families will prevail over speculative projects.

33. Depending on studies, figures vary about the number of hours spent by children in front of the television set, but it is undisputable that television has more hours for teaching the children than school teachers and parents have. The power of images and sound has been well documented. The results of many studies on damages to the brain by new cultural patterns are reported by Joseph Chilton Pearce, *Evolution's End: Claiming the Potential of Our Intelligence*. Harper San Francisco, 1992. Damages resulting from TV during childhood are pointed out: "the major damage of television has little to do with content: Its damage is neurological, and it has indeed damaged us, perhaps beyond repair" p. 164; see also pp. 165-167. George Gerbner, an authority on violence and television, estimates that the average American child will have watched 8,000 murders on television by the age of twelve. (*The Atlantic Monthly*, May 1997: "The Man Who counts the Killings" by Scott Stossel).

34. Josephine Alexander, a long time San Francisco newspaper writer, in her book *America Through the Eye of my Needle*, Dial Press, 1981, describes how the family becomes subordinated to the corporation, and the break-up of living patterns because of transfers of individuals or the moving of whole plants or offices. p. 104 and sq.

35. The blockade of the coasts of Nicaragua during the Sandinista Government, or in 1996 the opinion on the immorality of making and possessing nuclear weapons, are two examples among many others.

36. Martin Buber, *I and Thou*, Charles Scribners, 1970, pp. 97-98

37. "Whereas disregard and contempt for human rights have resulted in barbarous acts which have outraged the conscience of mankind. . . ." "Whereas the peoples of the United Nations have in the Charter reaffirmed their faith in fundamental human rights, in the dignity and worth of the human person and in the equal rights of men and women and have determined to promote social progress and better standards of life in larger freedom . . ." (Preamble of the Universal Declaration of Human Rights, 1948).

38. John Kavanaugh. *Following Christ in a Consumer Society*. Orbis, 1981, 1991.

39. The result of these meetings and reflections is presented in an unpublished manuscript: Ken Butigan, Pace e Bene Center, *Walking on the Waters*.

40. Father Miguel d'Escoto, MM, took a one month leave of absence from his responsibilities as Minister of Foreign Affairs of Nicaragua, in order to fast.

Chapter Four: Seeds of Violence from Colonial Origin

41. In 1996, the Secretary of Interior himself, Mr. Bruce Babbitt wrote: "our history is scarred with examples of how politicians in Washington repeatedly violated their agreements with Native Americans. They broke treaties out of greed, ignorance or indifference . . ." (*Las Vegas Sun*, September 19, 1996).

42. Even after the Sentencing Reform Act of 1984, established in order to avoid disparities based on race, etc., in 1993 the Justice Department reported that in federal courts, on average, Blacks sentenced between 1/20/89 and 6/30/90 received sentences 41% longer than did Whites (Cap. U.L. Rev 23, p. 23). The U.S. Sentencing Commission revealed that in 1994, an estimated 2,714,000 juveniles were arrested, 29% were Blacks, 62% were Whites. Black juveniles comprised only 15% of the total juvenile population (*New England Journal of Criminal and Civil Confinement*, Winter 1997, p. 32).

43. They speak of Columbus' **invasion** and not of Columbus discovery of America.

44. In March 1998, the Milton S. Eisenhower Foundation released a report. This foundation continues the work of the Kerner commission appointed by President Johnson to probe the causes of rioting in urban America in the 1960s. After mentioning the racial progress that occurred in 3 decades, the report continues: "The rich are getting richer, the poor are getting poorer and minorities are suffering disproportionately. . . . The top 1% of Americans have more wealth

than the bottom 90%. The U.S. is first in the world among industrial-ized nations when it comes to wage inequality" (Michel Flechter, from *The Washington Post* reprinted in *Las Vegas Review Journal* 3/1/98).

45. I am still amazed to hear that the Secession from England is called a Revolution when the most accurate words are Secession or War of Independence. The Colonies became an independent Republic, but the culture continued to be one of a colony.

46. F. Merk, *Manifest Destiny and Mission in American History*. Knopf, 1963, p. 261. The expression Manifest Destiny" appeared only in the middle of the nineteenth century. The word "Divine Mission" was used from the beginning and comes from the Puritan origin of the settlers.

47. Quoted by Robert Crunden, *A Brief History of American Culture*. 1994, North Castle Books, pp. 3-4.

48. It seems that the *Number One Complex* has also relationships with the fears inscribed inside the human nature. I read it as a synergy of the religious motivations of the 'manifest destiny' with these deep human tendencies. General Lee Butler in the previously quoted address to the National Press Club (cf. note 14) speaks of the "culture of messianic believers infused with a sense of historic mission and schooled in unshakable articles of faith." General Butler speaks of the biological reasons for the need of supremacy in these words "The unbounded wantonness of their [the nuclear weapons] effects is a perfect companion to the urge to destroy completely. They play on our deepest fears and pander to our darkest instincts. They corrode our sense of humanity, numb our capacity for moral outrage, and make thinkable the unimaginable. What is anguishingly clear is that these fears and enmities are no respecter of political systems and values. They prey on democracies and totalitarian societies alike, shrinking the norms of civilized behavior and dimming the prospect for escaping the savagery so powerfully imprinted in our genetic code." Robert Jay Lifton and Greg Mitchell in *Hiroshima in America: Fifty Years of Denial*, Grosset/Putnam Book, 1955, go further: "The attraction [of nuclear weapons] is one of merging with a source of power rivaling that of any deity. There is the further sense that the nuclear deity, in conferring its omnipresence, protects one from death and thereby offers an imagined version of immortality. This embrace of death-conquering power is the essence of the psychology of nuclearism." (p. 303). The relationship between the manifest destiny, the number one complex and the nuclear addiction might be tighter than many thought on first reflection.

49. Robert Bellah and al, *Habits of the Heart,* Harper and Row, 1986, p. 28

Chapter Five: Individual and National Dreams

50. Each month gamblers in Las Vegas are freed of $500 millions!

51. The average salary of chief executives in 1960 was 12 times greater than the average wage for factory workers; by 1990 it was 70 times greater. cf. William Greider, *Who Will Tell the People: The Betrayal of American Democracy,* Simon and Schuster, 1992, p. 397. Figures show that in other economic aspects the gap is widening: the number of millionaires and billionaires grew, as grew the number of homeless.

52. Max Weber, *The Protestant Ethic and the Spirit of Capitalism,* Scribner, 1958.

53. Of special interest is the book by Francoise Burgess, *America, le Rêve Blessé,* Autrement, 1992, with the collaboration of 18 well known authors, mainly Americans.

Chapter Six: An Individualistic Role Model, the "Self-made Man"

54. This text will use the term **man** deliberately to emphasize the gender dimension of the American model of success. Women are not automatically protected against this prevalent self-made model, even though they may not fall into it. Women and men as well, who have respected the feminine part of themselves (the anima) are not at ease with this model, a by-product of an hypertrophic masculine development (animus).

55. Robert Bellah and al, op.c. p. 143

56. Robert Bellah and al, op.c. p. 142

57. 1 Corinthians, chapter 13

58. This has been said many times, but lately Carver T. Yu in *Being and Relation,* Scottish Academic Press, Edinburg, 1987, summarizes it well. "One's identity is revealed and fulfilled in and through involvement with that which is other than oneself. This is why 'reality' cannot be expressed purely in terms of things, but has to be expressed in terms of events of encounter. This again explains why biblical man has his focus on historical events." Also in his *Pastoral Letter, Advent 1995,* the Archbishop of Adelaide, Australia, and his diocesan pastoral team write: "Humans are created by God as social beings. That is, if we do not enter into supportive and co-operative relations with others, we can neither live properly nor develop our gifts and potential" (cf, Pastoral *Constitution on the Church in the Modern World,* no. 12 and *Dogmatic Constitution on the Church,* II, no. 9, both from the Council Vatican II).

59. The French writer Christian Bobin in his famous book *Le Tres Bas* (*The Very Low*), portrays Francis of Assisi, following the example of Jesus Christ as the Very Low God revealing the immensity of the Almighty's love. Love supposes humbleness. Unfortunately the English translators did not respect this powerful title.

60. Alexis de Tocqueville, *Democracy in America*, Anchor Books. p. 513

61. Some authors have advanced that American individualism is a myth and should not be confused with localism and autonomy. cf. Barry Alan Shain, *The Myth of American Individualism*, Princeton University Press, 1996. "These two (Tocqueville and Chevalier) talented authors had confused America's localism, communalism, and particularism with social and political individualism." (p. 91). See also pp. 85 - 91. Some people may confuse these. Robert Bellah avoids this mistake and his opinion seems very convincing. My observations concur with Bellah's and Putnam's scientific research.

62. Charles Taylor, *Ethics of Authenticity*, Harvard University Press, 1991

63. op. cit. p. 2

64. op. cit. p. 17

65. cf. John Kavanaugh, *Following Christ in a Consumer Society*. Orbis 1981, 1991

66. Robert Bellah elaborates on "the continuing theme in American literature, of the hero who must leave society, alone or with one or a few others, in order to realize the moral good in the wilderness, at sea, or in the margins of settled society." (p. 144) ". . . the cowboy, like the detective, can be valuable to society only because he is a completely autonomous individual who stands outside it. To serve society, one must be able to stand alone, not needing others, not depending on their judgement, and not submitting to their wishes. . . . One accepts the necessity of remaining alone in order to serve the group. And this obligation to aloneness is an important key to the American moral imagination (p. 146). See also the social sources of ambivalence, pages 147-150, especially regarding American individualism compatible with conformism.

Chapter Seven: Facing the Tangled Roots of Violence

67. cf. footnote #29.

68. The official name of the World Bank is International Bank for Reconstruction and Development [I.B.R.D.].

69. In the International Monetary Fund (I.F.M.) each country has a number of votes proportionate to the capital invested. The U.S.A. invested around 17% of the total of the funds.

70. Inside the Organization for Economic Cooperation and Development (O.E.C.D.), the U.S.A. seems to have been the main advocate for the suppression of barriers in the investments, which would give free rein to the strongest corporations. October 27, 1997 in Paris, 565 organizations from 68 countries gathered to denounce the preparation of the M.A.I.
71. *Newsweek*, September 14, 1998.
72. Nevertheless we should mention the conquest of part of Ireland by Great Britain, and the strange fiction considering for one and half century the Algerian land as part of the metropolitan French territory.
73. Rollo May, *Power and Innocence: A Search for the Sources of Violence*, Norton and Company, 1972. See chap. 6.
74. St. Francis of Assisi told his brothers not to own any property so as to avoid having to defend these from any attack. This would destroy the communion with other human beings.

Afterword
75. In 1906 in South Africa, Gandhi used the expression 'total revolution' pointing out the need for "constructive work." Vinoba and Jayaprakash Narayan (JP) worked according to this concept. Narayan Desai, who grew till 20 years of age in Gandhi's ashram, after working with Vinoba and JP Movement, founded the *Institute for Total Revolution*, in Vechi, Gujarat (India). cf. Narayan Desai, *Towards a Nonviolent Revolution*, Sarva Seva Sangh Prakashan, Rajghat, Varanasi, India.
76. cf. Dom Helder Camara, *Spiral of Violence*, Sheed and Ward.
77. INFACT organized successively boycotts of Nestle, General Electric, The Tobacco Companies advertising for children and teenagers, and a campaign against the practices of the hospital colossus Columbia/HCA. INFACT proclaims that health and environment are more important than profit of the corporations.
78. The Albanian majority uses the word Kosova when the Serbian minority says Kosovo.
79. The coffee marketing from Central America cooperatives grows successfully. There have been previous alternatives against the dehumanization: cf. Acorn a movement out of the welfare movement and various initiatives from the Peace churches.
80. Robert Bly, *The Sibling Society*, Addison-Wesley Publ. 1996 Robert Bly quotes "Television floods the infant brain with images at the very time his or her brain is supposed to learn to make images from within. Failing to develop imagery means having no imagination." (Joseph

Chilton Pearce, *Evolution's End: Claiming the Potential of Our Intelligence*, Harper San Francisco, 1992, pp. 165-167). These two authors give various examples of passivity resulting from the lack of contact with the unexpected coming from nature.

81. Alexis Carrel, in *Man the Unknown*, Harper and Brothers, 1935, pointed out the risk of atrophy of adaptability if the human being does not use his potentialities. See especially chap. 6: Adaptive Functions. Alexis Carrel received the Nobel Prize in medicine in 1912.

82. M.K. Gandhi, *Indian Home Rule*, chap. XVI

Suggested Reading

Bailie, Gil, *Violence Unveiled: Humanity at the Crossroads*, Crossroads, 1995.

Bellah, Robert et al., *Habits of the Heart*, Harper & Row, 1986.

Bly, Robert, *The Sibling Society*, Addison-Wesley Publ., 1996.

Buber, Martin, *I and Thou*, Charles Scribner's.

Burgess, Francoise, *America, le Rêve Blessé*. Autrement, Paris, 1992.

Camara, Dom Helder, *Spiral of Violence*, Sheed & Ward.

Carrel, Alexis, *Man the Unknown*, Harper & Brothers, 1935.

Gandhi, M.K. *All Men Are Brothers*, World Without War Publications, 1972.

Girard, René, *Things Hidden Since the Foundation of the World*, Stanford University Press, 1987.

Girard, René, *Violence and the Sacred*, John Hopkins University Press, 1979.

Kavanaugh, John F. *Following Christ in a Consumer Society*, Orbis Press, 1981.

Lipton, Robert J. & Falk, Richard, *Indefensible Weapons: The Political and Psychological Case Against Nuclearism*, Basic Books, 1982.

May, Rollo, *Power and Innocence: A Search of the Sources of Violence*, Norton & Co., 1992.

Merk, F. *Manifest Destiny in American History*, Knopf, 1963.

Pearce, John Chilton, *Evolution's End: Claiming the Potential of our Intelligence*, Harpers of San Francisco, 1992.

Putnam, Robert, "Bowling Alone: American's Declining Social Capital," *Journal of Democracy*, January 1995.

Stossel, Scott, "The Man Who Counts the Killings," *Atlantic Monthly*, May, 1997.

Taylor, Charles, *Ethics of Authenticity*, Harvard University Press, 1991.

Tocqueville, Alexis de, *Democracy in America*, Anchor Books.

Yu, Carver T., *Being and Relation*, Scottish Academic Press, Edinburg, 1987.

Wachtel, Paul, *The Poverty of Affluence*, New Society Publishers, 1989.

Weber, May, *The Protestant Ethic and Spirit of Capitalism*, Scribner, 1958.

About the Author

Alain Richard's journey into nonviolence began in his native France. After graduation in Agronomy, Alain Richard joined the Franciscan Order in France. Having experienced the trauma of the Nazi culture, with others he explored nonviolent means during the Algerian war. During the Biafra and Bangladesh wars, he participated in nonviolent actions organized by the Ark Community. He also organized a group resisting payment of the percentage of income tax spent for military purposes in France.

Alain came to the U.S. in 1973 to serve as a Worker Priest. For six years he worked as a day laborer in Chicago alongside people of poverty coming from a mix of minority communities. Alain Richard experienced firsthand the economic violence endured by victims of structural injustice. In 1982, in the face of Cold War military buildups in the U.S. and the Soviet Union, he initiated a call for an International Fast for Peacemakers, organizing visible collective fasts in the Gandhian tradition, in preparation for the U.N. Second Session on Disarmament in New York. In the next several years, he was centrally involved in organizing fasts and hunger strikes in New York, San Francisco, Washington, D.C., Panama, and Guatemala.

In 1983, Alain was invited to be part of a Peace Brigades International team to study the feasibility of a PBI mission in Guatemala. During several periods of service with PBI in Guatemala from 1983 to 1985, he gave presentations on Gandhian nonviolence to religious leaders, worked with Grupo de Apoyo Mutuo (GAM) in planning public demonstrations, helped initiate the accompaniment program with endangered members of GAM, and facilitated communication about tortures and killings to the outside world, causing international outcry and demonstrations in Guatemala City with international support. In theses activities he faced threats and intimidation.

In 1989 Alain co-founded Pace e Bene, a Franciscan Service in Nonviolence located in Las Vegas, Nevada, and Berkeley, California. Since then he has made frequent presentations on nonviolence and social transformation at retreats and workshops, facilitated numerous nonviolence trainings, and written articles and pamphlets on nonviolence and cultural transformation. He has also lectured on nonviolence in Europe, Central and South America, and Australia. Alain follows the Gandhian tradition of valuing manual work; he is a skilled craftsman, mounting traditional icons on wood.

Booklets:
    Concerning Nonviolence and the Franciscan Movement
    Faith and Strategy in Nonviolent Actions
    Market Culture and Sacredness: Reflections on Violence and
        Nonviolence in a Market Dominated World
        (in collaboration with Peter Ediger)